Phebe Lankester

Wild Flowers worth Notice

For their beauty, associations, or uses

Phebe Lankester

Wild Flowers worth Notice
For their beauty, associations, or uses

ISBN/EAN: 9783337107031

Printed in Europe, USA, Canada, Australia, Japan

Cover: Foto ©ninafisch / pixelio.de

More available books at **www.hansebooks.com**

WILD FLOWERS
WORTH NOTICE

FOR THEIR BEAUTY
ASSOCIATIONS
OR USES

BY

M<small>RS</small> LANKESTER

<small>AUTHOR OF "BRITISH FERNS"</small>

*WITH 104 COLOURED FIGURES
FROM DRAWINGS BY J. E. SOWERBY*

LONDON   MDCCCXCVI
JAMES SHIELLS & CO.

Previous Editions published elsewhere.

PREFACE.

The success which has attended my little book on 'Wild Flowers worth Notice,' in the various forms in which for several years it has appeared before the public, determined the publisher to produce it again in a revised and improved condition, yet retaining its old character, only adding to it, rather than altering it. I am therefore glad to have the opportunity of correcting any error which may now exist in work done some years ago, and have endeavoured to bring the information given, up to the present time. When I first undertook the task I felt the difficulty of selecting from the British Flora certain 'Wild Flowers worth Notice,' and the task would be scarcely easier now were I called upon to make this selection definite. For what flowers are not worth notice? As, however, this cannot pretend to be an exhaustive treatise on the British Flora, such as exists in many forms and in large ponderous volumes compiled by profound and learned botanists, I have endeavoured to choose such plants as are representatives of particular families, and are remarkable either for their beauty of appearance or useful properties, and to give the best botanical description I can either find or make of them, so as to insure their recognition with the aid of the plate, and to add such traditions, legends, and poetical fancies, as are associated with them, in order to increase the interest with which they may be regarded.

Longfellow well says—

> "Wondrous truths, and manifold as wondrous,
> God hath written in the stars above;
> But not less in the bright flow'rets under us
> Stands the revelation of His love."

Then the natural connection between wild flowers and bright sunshine, or the first warm days of spring, does it not recall many a pleasant ramble to those who are in the enjoyment of youth and health? And even to the feeble or afflicted, the remembrance of the soft lulling influence of a summer's day, in sweet rural scenes, when everything seems joyous and yet tranquil, is a refreshment and a delight. In a charming series of short essays, called 'The Recreations of a Country Parson,' is one 'Concerning Summer Days,' which is so full of pleasant thoughts and the love of green trees and fields, hedges and hedge-rows, that I cannot but wish he would also write 'Concerning Wild Flowers.' When I first began to write of 'Wild Flowers,' it was suggested to me that I should select only those susceptible of cultivation; but to me, the great charm of the whole subject is to fancy the beautiful creatures in their natural homes, where they love to grow, not where they are artificially placed and tended by the hand of man. The wild bryony and clematis climbing luxuriantly over hedge and neighbouring tree—none the less rich for the demands made upon it by groups of happy smiling children for wreaths and festoons of wonderful length. The blue forget-me-not peeping out from its bed of green leaves by the bank of the clear running stream, asking only for moisture to fringe its sides with turquoise flowers. A hundred other lovely "children of the earth," as the blind girl of Bulwer calls them, owe much of their charm to the "lap" from which they spring—fresh and untouched by the hand of man. Not that I would in any manner depreciate the gardener's art or the skill of the florist, in so tending and cultivating even our native plants, as to produce such perfection of colour and symmetry of form, that it is difficult to recognize our friends of the wayside in the beauties of the garden. But this is surely the admiration with which we regard the well-dressed and fashionable denizens of a city in contrast with the more simple, but, perhaps, not less refined, rustic beauties. Then these favourites of ours must be sought for,—they call forth the energy and self-denial of their admirers, and while making great demands in the shape of country walks, and mountain rambles, bestow on their captors rosy cheeks, the inestimable prize of healthful and vigorous frames.

I have often, when urging the necessity of long walks and frequent exercise, been told by young folks living in the midst of rustic lanes, "There is no object to go out for. In cities and towns there are a hundred objects, and we are thus beguiled into walking." Why not then secure an object, if but one, for a country walk; an object which will unfailingly repay you and be cheering in the remembrance? Cultivate an acquaintance with the wild flowers of your own district, study them, gather them, transplant them if you will into a corner of your own garden; but, above all, visit them in their own homes, and be not satisfied till you have made a tolerable friendship with most of our British plants. Like all things of beauty, they perish quickly; and though each month of the year brings its own attractions with it, from the snowdrop of the early spring to the mistletoe and lichen of dark December, the lover of flowers will like to preserve the forms of as many favourites as possible, by drying; and few who have botanized in youth, cannot moralize in maturer age over the remembrances thus furnished, and few who have once engaged in collecting plants ever lose the recollection of the study or the interest it inspired. I therefore say to all, observe, collect, and preserve the wild flowers you find; arrange and name them scientifically, if possible; but if that be not in your power, still they will always be interesting to you as a pleasing record of "times and places, and old familiar faces," which one day you will value. When you have become well acquainted with the wild plants of your own neighbourhood, there are always *rare ones* to look for, and great is the interest and excitement attending the discovery of a rare species in an unexpected locality; but before you can expect to become a discoverer, you must be a tolerable botanist. But Botany, like other sciences, requires earnest and systematic study. Those who wish to be able to discover the name of a plant by the aid of botanical books, must first thoroughly understand the structure of a plant. Facilities for the study of Botany, both in the metropolis and in the provinces, are much greater now than when I first wrote this little book, and urged it upon young people of both sexes. The Government recognize Botany as one of the subjects for science teaching; and we find in the Syllabus for the examination of teachers issuing from the schools of science at Kensington, 'Subject XV., Elementary Botany, including questions on the chemistry of plants, histology, and the general structure of the flowering plant.' In an advanced course of the same subject we have an examination in vegetable physiology and morphology, Subject XVII. according to the Government Syllabus. But these efforts of the Government are simply in the way of examinations to test the knowledge of teachers who are supposed to have qualified themselves elsewhere, and to submit to this test of their fitness for teaching the subject in the board and other schools of the country. About 1500 candidates present themselves annually for examination, and Botany is now recognized as one of the subjects to be taught in our national schools. I am reminded of the efforts of the late Rev. Professor Henslow in this direction, long before the matter had ever been considered by public bodies and functionaries.

He was Professor of Botany in the University of Cambridge, and at the same time Rector of Hitcham, in Suffolk. The interest he took in his parish schools induced him to think that the girls might with advantage know something of the plants and vegetation of their own village. With his characteristic energy and goodness, he set about teaching all who chose to learn the elements of Botany, and by the encouragement of his own kindly smile and approving words, he soon succeeded in establishing a genuine love for plants, not only to *look at*, but to *understand*, in the minds of these children. The good professor arranged for his pupils a system of naming, classifying, and drying their specimens, and but few girls in the village of Hitcham are now unacquainted with their native plants. A good collection, made, dried, and named by these young botanists, may be inspected any day in the permanent scientific collection of the educational department of the South Kensington Museum, where it is deposited as an example and an encouragement to other village schools. It is but right to add that the testimony of the Inspectors of Schools goes to prove that this school ranks far above the average of schools in the district in every respect; and that in no way is there any difference in its rules or arrangements, with the exception of the introduction of Botany. We can, perhaps, readily account for the indirect influence of this study on the habits and minds of the pupils. The attention it awakens, the methods of arrangement and order it encourages, and the accuracy it necessitates, must re-act, in a great measure, on the whole character and thoughts of the learner.

With regard to the means at the disposal of a student for learning Botany, I may say that in London every medical school has its classes which are open to all young men who desire to study the subject, be they destined for the medical profession or not, and there are ladies' classes innumerable in association with every scheme for the improved education of women. At Bedford College, York Place, Portman Square, London, a larger and more complete course of lectures on Botany than can be obtained anywhere else is given to ladies by Mr. A. W. Bennett. It includes structural and physiological Botany, and extends over the whole session of study, numbering about 60 lectures. The fees are very moderate, and the teaching I know is excellent. There is also a ladies' class for the study of Botany about to be formed at University College, under the valuable guidance of the Rev. George Henslow, the son of the Professor whom I have mentioned, and who follows in his father's footsteps in the enthusiasm with which he regards his favourite science.

In all our provincial towns there are good and painstaking botanists, many of whom have already formed classes for work and study, and others who would I am sure be glad to give private instruction where such help is desired.

Let it not be supposed, however, that this search after wild flowers need be confined to such as have at their disposal all the appliances of science. The poorest inhabitant of a cottage has within her reach the same delight from this pursuit as the lady of the mansion, and we have many instances of the successful cultivation of Botany by those who have to labour hard for their daily bread. Among the hills which surround the great manufacturing city of the north, Manchester, and even within the very atmosphere of its smoke, there exists, at this day, a club of working naturalists—chiefly botanists. All of them are artisans in some one of the great factories of the district. An account published by one of themselves of their weekly botanical excursions, their field days, and the healthful and exhilarating effect on the minds and bodies of the members of this club, is most encouraging and delightful. The actual longevity of these humble naturalists is very remarkable. Old Crowther, one of the earliest workers in this direction, died at the age of 79; he was a simple-hearted man, willing to travel any distance and undergo any fatigue so that he secured his flower. As one of his old companions said, "he was not *learned*, but he was very *loving*." He never touched his wages for the purpose of botanical pleasure, but took home every penny, and trusted to fortunate accidents for the means of supplying his scientific wants. An account of the life and labours of another of this noble fraternity, the late Samuel Gibson, of Hebden Bridge, appeared in the 'Manchester Guardian' of the 30th May, 1849. His herbarium of plants was sold after his death for the sum of £75, and many portions of his collection are now to be seen in the Peel Park Museum, Salford. In 1858 an annual meeting of these working-men naturalists took place near Manchester, at which there mustered not less than 200 zealous and well-informed botanists, all, with the exception of four or five, of the artisan class. The one striking feature of this meeting seems to have been the hale and hearty appearance of the men already advanced in life; they were fine specimens of youth carried on into old age. There is evidently something in natural history wonderfully promotive of length of days. Men never step into the presence of nature with affection and reverence, but they come back blessed and strengthened with a reward.

Since Dr. Smiles undertook to write the biography of some of our remarkable working-men, we find that the love and study of plants, even to a scientific acquaintance with them, is a noticeable feature in their pursuits and self-education. But there are many who, having perhaps neither time nor opportunity for special oral instruction in Botany, are anxious to gain such knowledge of its principles as may be obtained from books. To such I recommend the following as best suited to their purpose:—Henfrey's 'Rudiments of Botany,' Hooker's 'Primer of Botany,' Oliver's 'Lessons in Elementary Botany,' Hooker's 'Student's Flora.' Babington's 'Manual of Botany' is a useful book of reference when the structure of plants has been mastered, and there are innumerable others which will answer the same purpose. For a large and comprehensive collection of the whole British Flora, beautifully illustrated with a coloured drawing of every plant, a minute scientific description, and a popular account of the history and legends attached to each, I may mention the beautiful work in eleven quarto volumes called 'English Botany,' published by Hardwicke, 192 Piccadilly. But this great work is above the reach of most, as its lowest price is £22 8s. It can, however, be taken in 83 Parts at 5s. each. I had the pleasure of being intimately connected with this interesting work, for the ten years it was in progress. A series of lectures has been published by the Examiners in Science in the Department of Education, "addressed to teachers on preparation for obtaining science certificates, and the method of teaching a science class." To the one on Botany, price 2d., I would specially refer, as explaining and amplifying much that I should wish to say here on the nature and advantages of this study. A Directory, price 6d., is also published, containing minute particulars as to regulations for establishing and conducting science classes in schools. Either of these pamphlets may be obtained by application to the Secretary of the Science and Art Department, South Kensington Museum. The late Rev. Professor Henslow, ever anxious to assist and gratify others at any personal sacrifice, sent me some years ago, in spite of the severe and painful illness which carried him off, a little pamphlet prepared as a companion to the specimens of his school plants deposited in the Kensington Museum, entitled 'Illustrations to be Employed in Practical Lessons on Botany.' In it he gives full particulars of the system he has pursued in his schools at Hitcham, and every direction for the commencement of the study of Botany, with little wood-cuts as unmistakable guides. Nearly every book on botany contains directions as to drying plants, and in my 'Plain and Easy Account of British Ferns,' I have endeavoured to be as clear as possible on this point. Here, therefore, I would only say to those who wish to make a collection of dried plants, get a 'Botanist's Portable Collecting Press.'* Change your paper often while your plants are drying; when dry, put them down carefully with bits of gummed paper on foolscap sheets; write the name, order, locality, and date of finding neatly underneath. It is a good plan to have a sheet of thick cartridge or brown paper for each family, to enclose all the specimens belonging to that family. You can then place these cases on shelves, in drawers, or a portfolio, for safety and preservation. Thus much pleasure is laid up for days when out-of-door excursions are impossible, but when the mind can be refreshed and interested by the recollection of scenes and localities of

---

* These presses are made in three sizes, costing 7s. 6d., 8s. 6d., 10s. 6d., and may be obtained from the publisher of this work.

which these dried and perhaps withered flowers are the only existing souvenirs. Wordsworth, the poet of nature, tells us truly that

> " Nature never did betray
> The heart that loved her! 'Tis her privilege,
> Through all the years of this our life, to lead
> From joy to joy!"

P. L.

INTRODUCTION.

This little volume certainly does not presume to be a work on Botany, strictly so called, of which there are so many and such exhaustive guide-books to the British Flora. It is not my intention to describe each Natural Order or Family to which our specimens belong. Nearly every reader who is sufficiently interested in plants to care to look for them, and to compare them with the plates and descriptions here given, will already know what constitutes a family or natural order; but lest some one should take up this book who has not given any previous attention to the subject, I would say that the whole vegetable kingdom is divided into three great classes. These, again, are subdivided into orders, families, or tribes, according as they most resemble each other; these are again subdivided into genera, and again into species. We may popularly explain the system of classifying thus:—In a library there shall be a number of volumes of all sizes, shapes, and containing varieties of matter; we agree to classify them not only by size and colour, but according to their contents. Take all those treating of chemistry, then all those on botany; let those be families or orders; then all the red-bound chemical books,—that is a genus; then from those separate the volumes with gilt leaves of a certain size, and those with marbled leaves of a certain size,—these constitute species. In this way have our great botanists divided the vegetable kingdom for the convenience of arrangement and study; and although there are often differences of opinion as to what shall constitute a *species* or a *variety*, which would correspond in a library to a red, gilt-edged book, with a slight change of style in the cover, say with a thicker, stouter back than the rest; yet in the main there is but little difficulty in preserving order and in classifying every known plant according to its peculiarities. It is very necessary for any one who wishes to study Botany to understand thoroughly the distinguishing points of each natural order. When once these are fixed in the mind, it is easy to recognize plants as belonging to certain families, and from the established habits of the family to draw conclusions as to the nature, locality, and properties of the specimen under notice. In order to give some notion of the nature of a Natural Order or Family, I think it well to give a sketch of that to which our first specimen belongs, and which comes first in nearly all works on Botany.

RANUNCULACEÆ.—The plants belonging to this order are herbs or climbing plants, never shrubs or trees. The flowers are solitary, that is, singly, on a stalk, or in racemes, that is, in bunches of irregular flowerets. The petals are generally five, but sometimes are deformed and very minute, or wanting altogether. The stamens are very numerous, and placed on the receptacle. The fruit is composed of several carpels, distinct or partially united. The seeds are erect or pendulous. The family *Ranunculaceæ* are widely diffused all over the globe, but especially in cool and temperate climates. Within the tropics they are chiefly confined to high mountain districts. They are remarkable for their acrid, poisonous qualities in many of the species of *Ranunculus;* the acrid secretion in the leaves will produce blisters if applied to the skin; whilst the Aconite or Monk's Hood is a deadly poison. A good example of the chief characteristics of the family is afforded by the species figured in our Plate No. 1.

SYSTEMATIC CHAPTER OF CONTENTS.

FLOWERING PLANTS.

CLASS I.

EXOGENS OR DICOTYLEDONS.

Subdivision I.—THALAMIFLORÆ.

ORDER 1.—RANUNCULACEÆ.

	PAGE
Ranunculus bulbosus ..	1
Clematis Vitalba	2
Anemone nemorosa	3
Adonis autumnalis	4
Trollius Europæus	5
Aquilegia vulgaris	6
Aconitum Napellus	7
Caltha Palustris	8

ORDER 2.—NYMPHÆACEÆ.

	PAGE
Nymphæa alba	10
Nuphar lutea	12

ORDER 3.—PAPAVERACEÆ.

	PAGE
Papaver Argemone	13
Glaucium luteum	15

ORDER 4.—CRUCIFERÆ.

	PAGE
Isatis tinctoria	17
Draba verna	18
Nasturtium officinale	19

ORDER 5.—CISTACEÆ.

	PAGE
Helianthemum vulgare ..	22

ORDER 6.—VIOLACEÆ.

	PAGE
Viola odorata	22
Viola tricolor	24

ORDER 7.—DROSERACEÆ.

	PAGE
Drosera rotundifolia	26
Parnassia palustris	37

ORDER 8.—CARYOPHYLLACEÆ.

	PAGE
Dianthus Caryophyllus ..	29
Lychnis diurna	30

ORDER 9.—LINACEÆ.

	PAGE
Linum usitatissimum	31

ORDER 10.—MALVACEÆ.

	PAGE
Lavatera arborea	32
Malva moschata	33
Althæa officinalis	34

xviii SYSTEMATIC CHAPTER OF CONTENTS.

	PAGE		PAGE
ORDER 11.—HYPERICACEÆ.		ORDER 12.—GERANIACEÆ.	
Hypericum calycinum	35	Geranium sanguineum	38
		Geranium Robertianum	39
		Oxalis Acetosella	41

Subdivision II.—CALYCIFLORÆ.

	PAGE		PAGE
ORDER 13.—LEGUMINOSÆ.		ORDER 17.—CUCURBITACEÆ.	
Ulex Europæus	42	Bryonia dioica	59
Ononis spinosa	45		
Trifolium fragiferum	46	ORDER 18.—CRASSULACEÆ.	
Lathyrus aphaca	53	Sempervivum Tectorum	60
ORDER 14.—ROSACEÆ.		ORDER 19.—SAXIFRAGACEÆ.	
Rosa Canina	47	Saxifraga Hirculus	61
Rosa spinosissima	52	Chrysosplenium alternifolium	63
Potentilla reptans	54		
		ORDER 20.—UMBELLIFERÆ.	
ORDER 15.—ONAGRACEÆ.		Sium Angustifolium	62
Epilobium angustifolium	55	Hydrocotyle vulgaris	64
Œnothera biennis	56	Eryngium maritimum	64
		Crithmum maritimum	66
ORDER 16.—LYTHRACEÆ.		ORDER 21.—RUBIACEÆ.	
Lythrum Salicaria	58	Galium Assarine	67

Subdivision III.—COROLLIFLORÆ.

	PAGE		PAGE
ORDER 22.—LORANTHACEÆ.		ORDER 26.—COMPOSITÆ.	
Viscum album	69	Bellis perennis	79
		Cichorium Intybus	82
ORDER 23.—CAPRIFOLIACEÆ.		Aster Tripolium	83
Sambucus nigra	73	Inula Helenium	84
Lonicera Periclymenum	74	Anthemis nobilis	85
ORDER 24.—GALIACEÆ.		ORDER 27.—CAMPANULACEÆ.	
Galium verum	76	Campanula rotundifolia	86
ORDER 25.—DIPSACEÆ.		ORDER 28.—ERICACEÆ.	
Dipsacus Fullonum	77	Vaccinium Myrtillus	88

SYSTEMATIC CHAPTER OF CONTENTS.

	PAGE
Erica Tetralix	89
Calluna vulgaris	90

ORDER 29.—AQUIFOLACEÆ.

Ilex aquifolium	92

ORDER 30.—GENTIANACEÆ.

Gentiana verna	94
Menyanthes trifoliata	95

ORDER 31.—CONVOLVULACEÆ.

Convolvulus sepium	96
Convolvulus Soldanella	97

ORDER 32.—BORAGINACEÆ.

Echium vulgare	98
Myosotis palustris	99

ORDER 33.—SOLANACEÆ.

Hyoscyamus niger	102
Atropa Belladonna	104
Solanum Dulcamara	107

ORDER 34.—SCROPHULARIACEÆ.

Veronica Chamædrys	108
Antirrhinum majus	110
Verbascum Thapsus	111

ORDER 35.—LABIATÆ.

Scutellaria Galericulata	113
Nepeta Glechoma	114

ORDER 36.—LENTIBULACIÆ.

Utricularia vulgaris	115

ORDER 37.—PRIMULACEÆ.

Glaux maritima	116
Primula vulgaris	116
Primula officinalis	117
Lysimachia nummularia	119
Anagallis arvensis	119

ORDER 38.—PLANTAGINACEÆ.

Plantago major	120

Subdivision IV.—MONOCHLAMYDEÆ.

ORDER 39.—EUPHORBIACEÆ.

Euphorbia Peplis	122

ORDER 40.—CALLITRICHACEÆ.

Callitriche verna	123

ORDER 41.—URTICACEÆ.

Urtica Dioica	124

CLASS II.

ENDOGENS OR MONOCOTYLEDONS.

ORDER 42.—DIOSCOREACEÆ.

	PAGE
Tamus communis	126

ORDER 43.—HYDROCHARIDACEÆ.

Stratiotes Aloides	127

ORDER 44.—ORCHIDACEÆ.

Orchis mascula	128
Orchis militaris	129
Ophrys apifera	130
Ophrys muscifera	131

ORDER 45.—IRIDACEÆ.

Iris Pseudacorus	132

ORDER 46.—AMARYLLIDACEÆ.

Narcissus Pseudonarcissus	134

ORDER 47.—LILIACEÆ.

	PAGE
Hyacinthus nonscriptus	136
Muscari racemosum	137
Scilla verna	138
Fritillaria meleagris	138
Lilium Martagon	139
Colchicum autumnale	140

ORDER 48.—ALISMACEÆ.

Butomus umbellatus	142
Sagittaria sagittifolia	143

ORDER 49.—ARACEÆ.

Arum maculatum	144

ORDER 50.—CYPERACEÆ.

Eriophorum Angustifolium	146
Scirpus lacustris	147
Acorus Calamus	149

WILD FLOWERS.

BUTTERCUP, OR BULBOUS CROWFOOT.

RANUNCULUS BULBOSUS.

THE name Buttercup is familiarly applied to nearly all the species of Ranunculus with bright yellow flowers. This species is distinguished from the rest by its thickened stem, which at the lower part, under the ground, expands into a sort of bulb, and by the sepals, which, as soon as the flower expands, are reflexed or turned back on the peduncle. The leaves are divided into three stalked segments, more or less cut. The whole plant is about a foot high; it flowers in the early summer, and is abundant in our meadows and waste places. In Scotland it is found southwards; but in the north is seldom to be seen. The genus Ranunculus is the type of the natural order Ranunculaceæ. The species are generally acrid, and not eaten by cattle in their growing state.

TRAVELLERS' JOY—OLD MAN'S BEARD, OR VIRGIN'S BOWER.

CLEMATIS VITALBA.

CLEMATIS VITALBA belongs to an almost exceptional genus of the Ranunculus family. Its stem is climbing, and woody at the base; it is the only British plant which gives us some faint notion of the bush ropes of the tropics. The woody stems sometimes attain a great thickness, and the petioles or leaf-stalks of the young branches act as tendrils, and cause it to spread to a great extent over trees and shrubs in its neighbourhood. The flowers are of a greenish-white colour, in loose bunches. The carpels are very conspicuous when ripe, from their persistent styles, which grow into long feathery awns; hence the name, Old Man's Beard. The petals are absent in this species, the flowers being formed by the sepals. The leaves are pinnate; the leaflets, usually five in number, ovate and slightly pointed in shape. This pretty and slightly sweet-scented plant is one of the greatest ornaments of our country hedges; and we can, doubtless, all remember with pleasure the delight with which in our summer rambles we have torn down long wreaths of its pretty green leaves and pale flowers to adorn a rustic head-dress, or to luxuriate in its fragrance, which it possesses in some degree in common with its relation *C. Flammula,* the deliciously fragrant plant so well known in our gardens.

There are above a hundred species of Clematis, most of which are favourite plants in cultivation. Both our own British species, *Clematis Vitalba* and *C. crispa* (an exotic species), have been used as rubefacients in rheumatism, and the dried leaves of *C. Vitalba* form fodder for cattle in some places, the acrid juice they contain when green disappearing after drying. When dried, boys use clematis wood for smoking as they do ratan. A thin slice of the wood is an interesting object under the microscope, from the curious manner in which the parts of the stem are arranged.

WOOD ANEMONE, OR WIND FLOWER.

ANEMONE NEMOROSA.

This is one of our commonest and prettiest hedge-plants, belonging to the same order, Ranunculaceæ. The whole of the anemones are lowly herbs, usually perennial, as is this species. The flowers are solitary, consisting of six smooth white elliptical sepals. The leaves consist of three ovate or lanceolate leaflets, of a dark bright-green colour. The flowers may be seen in or near woods as soon in the year as April, and our earliest spring walks are often gladdened by its presence. Nothing can be prettier than a bouquet of these simple delicate white flowers in the midst of their natural guardians, the dark finely-cut green leaves; they are among the earliest harbingers of the season,

> When earth, exulting from her wintry tomb,
> Breaks forth with flowers.

To see these delicate flowers in perfection, however, we must choose for our woodland excursion a bright unclouded day, for the Wood Anemone is a natural barometer, and droops at the approach of rain. There are several British species of anemone; but we have selected the *A. Nemorosa* as the most attractive from its very simplicity.

Anemone Pulsatilla, has fine large purple flowers. *A. Pæonia*, the Peacock Anemone, common in the south of Europe, with its bright scarlet or scarlet and white flowers; and *A. Coronaria*, the garden Anemone, with its many varieties of hue, form striking contrasts to the unobtrusive appearance of our little favourite. The whole genus partake of the acrid and poisonous qualities of the family, and are unsafe to take, even as medicines, although they have had a reputation in various complaints.

PHEASANT'S EYE.

ADONIS AUTUMNALIS.

ADONIS AUTUMNALIS—Pheasant's Eye—partakes more of the character of the true Ranunculus than any plant we have yet described; it is distinguished from that genus by the absence of a little scale at the base of the petals, and from other genera of the same order by the numerous hard, dry, sharp-pointed grains of which its fruit consists. It is an upright annual plant, from eight inches to a foot in height. The leaves are finely cut into numerous narrow linear segments. The sepals are green or slightly coloured; the petals from five to eight in number, but slightly longer than the calyx, of a bright scarlet colour, with a dark or black spot at the base inside the flower. It is constantly to be found in cornfields in the summer, from May to September, in England and Ireland, and sometimes in Scotland.

GLOBE FLOWER.

TROLLIUS EUROPÆUS.

TROLLIUS EUROPÆUS, Globe Flower, belongs also to the order Ranunculaceæ, and is so called from the German word *trollen*, round, in reference to the round shape of the flowers. The species are all perennial herbs, with divided leaves and yellow flowers, composed of coloured sepals. It is not a large genus, and our native species, *Trollius Europæus*, is the most generally known. It has from ten to fifteen broad concave sepals, usually turned over in the shape of a ball, and concealing petals, stamens, and carpels.

In Scotland it is called Lucken Gowan, or Cabbage Daisy. In some parts of England, as well as on the continent of Europe, they are gathered on festive occasions for making garlands and decorating the cottages of the peasantry. In common with its natural order, this plant is slightly acrid. It likes a rich, moist soil, but loves a good strong light to flourish under; deriving vigour and colour as the moon derives her light.

COLUMBINE.

AQUILEGIA VULGARIS.

AQUILEGIA, literally water-gatherer, is another genus of plants of the Ranunculus family, so called because the leaves collect water in their hollow. *A. Vulgaris*, the Common Columbine of our hedges, is a pretty little plant with a stem from one to two feet high or more. The flowers, which are curious, are of a dull purple or blue colour, and drooping. The root-leaves and those at the lower part of the stem grow in a large tuft, each with a long stalk. The petals have all a long curved horn or spur at their base, which projects below the calyx. The stamens are numerous. The English name, Columbine, is derived from a fanciful likeness to a dove, which is produced if we separate one petal from the flower-cluster; it brings with it two sepals, and the appearance of a dove may be imagined. When wild, the blossom is of a light-blue colour, but the plant is subject to great changes in cultivation, and readily produces double flowers. We find in 'Brown's British Pastorals,' that our dove-like plant was, in former times, the insignia of a deserted lover:—

> "The Columbine by lonely wand'rer taken,
> Is there ascribed to such as are forsaken."

MONK'S-HOOD, OR WOLF'S-BANE.
ACONITUM NAPELLUS.

ACONITUM NAPELLUS is a plant with a firm erect stem one and a half to two feet high, also belonging to the Ranunculaceæ. The leaves are either stalked or very close to the stem, of a dark-green colour and very smooth. The flowers are large, and are easily recognized as having the very large uppermost segment of the calyx overhanging the petals and other parts in the form of a helmet. The two upper petals inside this covering are long and narrow, with spurs; the three lower ones very small. We may all remember having plucked these flowers in our childhood, and, having thrown back the hood or calyx, have delighted in the fairy chariot and steeds formed by the petals thus set free. No vegetable poisons are more powerful than those produced by this genus of plants; and the common species, *A. Napellus*, yields it in the greatest degree. It is sometimes prescribed medicinally, and according to some writers very beneficially. From ancient times these plants have been celebrated as virulent poisons. In 1524 and 1526 two criminals at Rome and at Prague, to whom the root was given by way of experiment, very quickly perished. It entered into the deadly draught which the old men of Ceos were condemned to drink when they became infirm, and is also said to have been the principal ingredient in the cup which Medea prepared for Theseus. The most virulent Indian poison, *Bikh* or *Bish*, is supposed to be a preparation of a species of Aconite. Dr. Wallich describes *A. Ferox* as used by the native Indians to poison the water in the tanks, in order to impede the progress of a hostile army. It is also used to poison darts, arrows, and spears.

THE MARSH MARIGOLD.

CALTHA PALUSTRIS.

This plant is common enough by the side of any stream or ditch we pass in our country walks in the spring and summer. Its pretty golden cups have attracted the admiration of poets from very early times. John Dryden writes:—

> "And get soft hyacinths with iron blue
> To shade Marsh Marigolds of shining hue."

PLATE II.

MONK'S-HOOD. *Aconitum Napellus.*   MARSH MARIGOLD. *Caltha Palustrus.*
WHITE WATER LILY. *Nymphaea Alba.*   YELLOW WATER-LILY. *Nuphar Lutea.*
HORN-POPPY. *Glaucium luteum.*   PRICKLY POPPY. *Papaver Argemone.*

Belonging as it does to the order Ranunculaceæ it is often confounded with the buttercups, owing, perhaps, to its bright yellow colour; and some people think that the bright golden appearance of butter is owing to the presence of this flower in pasture-land. But cows will not eat it at all unless obliged to do so by extreme hunger, and even then they are often injured by it. In appearance the Marsh Marigold is like a large thick buttercup, with a stout stem and very large glossy leaves. It is a beautiful flower, and by the side of a river amidst the emerald grasses it shines like a golden vase. Shakespeare undoubtedly thought of its golden cups reflected in the clear river stream when he wrote the well-known lines—

> "Hark! hark the lark at heaven's gate sings,
> And Phœbus 'gins to rise,
> His steeds to water at those springs,
> On chaliced flowers that lies."

In common with most acrid and poisonous plants the Marsh Marigold possesses a certain old medical reputation. Dr. Withering believes in the exhalation of some potent qualities from the flowers, for he tells us that a girl was cured of fits by the introduction of a quantity of the flowers into her bed-room, and this reputation induced some who believed it to make an infusion of the plant and administer it to children as a cure for various kinds of fits. Such remedies appear to us very dangerous however.

The Marsh Marigold is also called Water Calthrops and Meadow Rout.

THE WHITE WATER-LILY.
NYMPHÆA ALBA.

THIS plant belongs to another natural order or family —Nymphæaceæ, which consists chiefly of aquatic herbs with floating leaves and solitary flowers; found in all temperate and tropical parts of the world. They have usually four sepals and many petals in several rows, contracting gradually into stamens. The fruits are numerous, but are either imbedded into the receptacle, or combined together to form a single ovary with many cells. *Nymphæa alba*, the White Water-Lily, has bright, smooth, heart-shaped leaves, floating on the surface of the water; usually six or eight inches in diameter. The flowers are large, white, and floating, with yellow stigmas. It is one of the brightest ornaments of our still lakes and ponds throughout Europe, and is a favourite plant with all lovers of flowers. The flower of the White Water-Lily is an excellent example of the law of morphology in plants. The doctrine that all the parts of a plant are modifications of the leaves, may be aptly illustrated by tracing the gradual changes which take place in the floral envelopes of this plant. Begin with the outermost whorl of sepals, and trace the leaf-like character gradually lessening until they become changed into perfect stamens, with petal-like anthers attached to them. The flower-stems are porous and succulent, but rapidly lose their moisture if removed from the water. The Water-Lily may be transplanted from its native home by placing the thick stems in baskets of earth, and fastening stones to them so as to keep them well under water. These stems have a bitter, astringent taste, but are quite free from any of the poisonous acrid principle of the last family of plants we met with. They have been used in dyeing a dark-brown colour. Goats and swine will eat them, and they have been used medicinally. It is, however, as an object of beauty that the Water-Lily claims our attention; and nothing can be more lovely than a calm lake on whose bosom may be seen floating numbers of these snowy nymphs. On Loch Lomond acres are covered with them; and in all the northern English lakes they are more or less abundant. Like the sacred Lotus of the Nile, the flowers rise and expand as the sun gains strength, and close again in the evening; sleeping as it were through the hours of darkness until called into life again by the warm rays of light.

Moore poetically describes this natural process—

> "Those virgin lilies all the night,
> Bathing their beauties in the lake,
> That they may rise more fresh and bright,
> When their beloved sun's awake."

The stimulus of the sun's rays seems to have relation to the fertilization of the plant. The pollen, if scattered beneath the water, would be washed away and decomposed, while on the expanded raised flower it is received without injury. This is truly the object for which—

> "The water-lily to the light
> Her chalice rears of silver white."

And as it is with poets in sentiment, so it should be in our every-day life; each daily duty, if viewed aright, contains in it the elements of poetry, which may be made to surround the most prosaic acts of existence with beauty.

YELLOW WATER-LILY.

NUPHAR LUTEA.

This beautiful water plant is familiar to all who have ever enjoyed a season of river life, or even to those who make occasional boating excursions on our rivers. It belongs to the same natural order as its more modestly attired sister the White Water-Lily, though of a different genus. " In golden armour glorious to behold," it forms a glorious object on the surface of lake or river, and is more frequently seen than the White Water-Lily. The golden blossom of this species has a powerful and not very refined smell resembling ardent spirits, hence it has the common name of Brandy-Bottle. The Greeks prepare a cordial from the flowers. Both the seeds and the root-stocks contain a quantity of starch, and the leaves have been used as a styptic. All parts of the plant contain tannin and are useful in the process of tanning. An infusion of the rootstock was long considered to be a specific in eruptive diseases of the skin. Many of the tropical species of Nymphæaceæ have wonderfully tinted and coloured blossoms of blue and crimson. The magnificent Water-Lily of the West, known as the *Victoria Regia*, is nearly allied to these British lilies. The flowers of this beautiful species are often fifteen feet in diameter, and its leaves measure six feet and a-half across. All lovers of floral beauty should not fail to see these magnificent flowers in the aquatic house in the Royal Gardens at Kew, or in the Regent's Park Botanical Gardens, where in the seasons they blossom in perfection, cultivated and encouraged by careful attention to imitate as much as possible their natural conditions and temperature.

PRICKLY POPPY.

PAPAVER ARGEMONE.

PAPAVER ARGEMONE belongs to the family of Poppies—Papaveraceæ. They are all herbs with much-divided leaves and no stipules. The sepals are two in number, and fall off as the flower expands The flower consists of four regular-shaped petals.

The stamens are distinct and numerous. The fruit is a capsule opening in valves; the seeds albuminous, and containing a fixed oil. *Papaver Argemone*, the Pale Poppy, or Prickly Poppy, is not so common as the Corn Poppy, *P. Rhœas;* but is remarkable for its delicacy. The flowers are of a pale red colour, with a dark spot at the base; the segments of the leaves are few and narrow, and the fruit or capsule is covered with minute bristles. There are several other species of British poppies: the common Field or Corn Poppy, *P. Rhœas;* the Long-headed Poppy, *P. Dubium;* the Rough Poppy, *P. Hybridum;* the Opium Poppy, or *P. Somniferum.* All the species exude more or less a milky juice, the narcotic properties of which are considerable only in *P. Somniferum.* This species yields the poppy-heads so commonly used in fomentations. Opium can be prepared from the juice of the English plant, which has been used instead of foreign opium; and although not so powerful in its action, possesses the same properties.

Many are the curious legends and traditions connected with the poppy plant. Theocritus tells us that the silken petals of the poppy prove talismans for Cupid, thus:—

> "By a prophetic *poppy-leaf* I found
> Your changed affection; for it gave no sound,
> Though in my hand struck hollow as it lay,
> But quickly wither'd like your love away."

In classic lore, the poppy was sacred to Ceres, though

our modern notions of agriculture would rather regard it as an intruder into her domains.

Of all the strange and baneful, as well as beneficial, effects of the poppy-juice or opium, we can hardly speak here. As a medicine it is most valuable, if carefully administered, and it has often soothed and palliated the sufferings of humanity. As a hurtful and sensual indulgence, its effects are well known; in Eastern countries, perhaps, better than our own. The fascination of this pernicious habit, and its terrible results, are vividly described in a popular work,— 'Confessions of an English Opium-eater.'

YELLOW HORN-POPPY.

GLAUCEUM LUTEUM.

This plant reminds us of our seaside holiday-time, of sandy beaches and rolling waves; and as with no objects are mental associations more vivid than with flowers, the sight of a plant but rarely met with, must recall to our minds the circumstances under which we first saw it. Perhaps a first visit to the sea-beach, or to some well-loved spot, and all the delicious refreshment of the sea-breeze, the rest and repose which steal over the most active mind when listening to the tune of the waters, is in a measure brought back again, as we see, even in its dead and dried state, the well-remembered plant of the sea-shore. Our Yellow Horn-Poppy is the most striking and remarkable of our sea-shore plants, and cannot fail to arrest the attention of the most casual observer, in a position where so little vegetation flourishes. The foliage is of a pale sea-green colour, which botanists term glaucous: hence its scientific name. It is rough, with short bristles; the pods or horns are from six to ten or twelve inches long, crowned by the spreading lobes of the stigma. When we see this pretty plant, it is interesting to remember the history of Glaucus, after whom it is named. He was the son of Neptune and of Nais, a sea-nymph, but lived on shore. His nature, however, had some influence on his habits, and he was fond of fishing. One day, having been very successful in his sport, he laid his scaly prize on a neighbouring marsh, when to his great surprise they began to nibble the green grass, and then

> "Sudden darting o'er the verdant plain,
> They spread their fins as in their native main,
> Left their new master, and regain'd the sea."

Amazed at what he saw, Glaucus resolved to test the power of the herbage in his own person; and no sooner had he bitten it, than his hereditary aquatic propensities seized him, and into the ocean he leaped, when, for his faith and courage, he was received as a denizen among the sea-gods.

In their domain he still shows his royal descent by wearing a golden robe; and yet, from old affection, high above it he bears his favourite long and curved fishrod, with its point bent, as if a captive fish ever strained it. Glaucus never goes far out to sea, but rather frequents the shores and cliffs; for Scylla, whom he loved, was turned into a rock, with howling waves around her; and his faithfulness retains him still close to her side.

The Yellow Horn-Poppy is the "squats" of the Portland Islanders.

DYER'S WOAD.

ISATIS TINCTORIA.

OUR next specimen belongs to another and very extensive and useful family of plants—Cruciferæ or Crossworts. The species are herbs, or rarely under-shrubs, with alternate leaves and no stipules; four sepals, four petals of equal size, or two on the outer-side layer. The stamens are six in number, of which two are generally shorter, or sometimes altogether absent. The fruit is a pod, divided into two cells by a thin partition, from which the valves generally separate when ripe. When long, it is called a silique, and when short, a silicle.

Isatis Tinctoria preserves the general characteristics of the family. The stem is from eighteen inches to two or three feet high, branched in the upper part.

Its long leaves are smooth and coarsely toothed and stalked, the pods hanging on slender stalks downwards. The flower is of a yellow colour.

The specific name *tinctoria* signifies its use in dyeing or staining. From it was undoubtedly obtained the blue dye or woad with which the Ancient Britons stained their skins.

When the arts of civilized life were not practised, this substance supplied, according to the poet Garth, all the requirements of a fashionable toilette.

> "In times of old when British nymphs were known
> To love no foreign fashions like their own,
> When dress was monstrous, and fig-leaves the mode,
> And quality put on no paint but woad."

At the present day this plant is used by dyers, not on account of its own blue colour, but as a mordant for other colours. Its colouring principle seems to be identical with indigo. It is cultivated in Bedfordshire, Northamptonshire, and Somersetshire.

THE COMMON WHITLOW-GRASS.

DRABA VERNA.

DRABA VERNA, a cruciferous plant, is one of our earliest spring flowers; and as soon as the bright days of March and April tempt us out into the fields and lanes, we may look for it on dry walls and banks, with

PLATE III.

DYER'S WOAD. *Isatis tinctoria.*
WATER-CRESS. *Nasturtium officinale.*
SWEET VIOLET. *Viola odorata.*

WHITLOW-GRASS. *Draba Verna.*
ROCK ROSE. *Helianthemum Vulgare.*
HEART'S EASE. *Viola tricolor.*

its little stalk of white flowers. It is a small annual plant, and lasts but for a few weeks; the leaves are all towards the base, ovate or oblong. The seed-pods burst open in the month of May, and scatter the seeds into the ground, where they lay securely till the next season. The tiny flowers droop at night to keep the stamens from the chilly dews of the early spring. The common name, Whitlow-grass, is given on account of the use of the leaves as a poultice in those unpleasant swellings.

It belongs to the genus *Erophila* of De Candolle, a pretty name, expressive of its early appearance.

COMMON WATER-CRESS.

NASTURTIUM OFFICINALE.

NASTURTIUM OFFICINALE—also known as *Sisymbrium Nasturtium*, the Common Water-cress—should be familiar to every one, as belonging to the family Cruciferæ. It is very likely to be confounded with a poisonous plant with which it grows, the Fool's Cress, as it is called (*Sium nodiflorum*). From this it may always be distinguished, and, in fact, from all other Umbelliferæ, by the petioles of the leaves not forming a sheath round the stem. In addition to the characters of the genus, the Water-cress is known principally by the form of its leaves. The leaf is composed of from five to seven leaflets, which are arranged opposite each other on a common leaf-stalk with a terminal leaflet. The leaflets are somewhat heart-shaped and slightly wavered or toothed; they are succulent and their surface is smooth. The terminal leaflet is always the largest. The petiole or leaf-stalk does not in any manner embrace the stem. The flowers are white, and the pods, when ripe, are about an inch long. It is a native of rivulets throughout the world, and is very plentiful in our own country. The ancient reputation of this plant as an article of food, valuable both for its pleasant pungent taste and its antiscorbutic properties, is well founded. Recent writers on the subject of diet have shown that in partaking of fresh uncooked vegetable food in the shape of salads or fruit, we are obtaining those salts of potash and other constituents so necessary to health, which in the process of cooking are dissolved away.* Water-cresses are said to contain iodine.

No better vehicle for the introduction of these important substances can there be than fresh bright Water-cresses; and our old friend Gerarde's notion of their value presages all the modern discoveries as to their virtue. He says that the eating of Water-cresses restores their wonted bloom to the cheeks of sickly young ladies. He might have added that a walk to the running stream where they grow would enhance the effects of the remedy. So large is the consumption

* See Dr. Lankester's 'Lectures on Food.' London: R. Hardwicke.

of Water-cresses in London that they are cultivated by market-gardeners to a great extent by means of artificial water-supplies; but none are so delicious as those from natural streams. Our popular street-cry has been rhymed by Swift thus:—

"Fine spring water-grass, fit for lad or lass."

The name *cress* has, according to writers, many origins. One says it signifies water *cross*, from its cruciate flowers. Chaucer employs the Saxon word *kers* (cress) to signify anything worthless:—

"Of paramours ne raught he not a kers."

From which, perhaps, is derived the phrase of not caring a curse for a thing. *Nasturtium* is a name given to all these biting plants, each being a *nasus tortus*, or nose-twitcher. Pliny records that they put the nose into convulsions. Long ago the refreshing nature of these plants as food was recognized, and there is a Greek proverb, "Eat cress to learn more wit." Knowing, as we now do, the influence of the physical over the mental, we can rationally understand the proverb.

There are several other species of Nasturtium native in England—the Creeping Cress, *N. Sylvestre* or *N. Palustre;* the Water-rocket, *N. Terrestre;* and the Water-radish, *N. Amphibium.*

THE ROCK ROSE, OR ROCK CIST.

HELIANTHEMUM VULGARE.

OUR next plant belongs to a new family—Cistaceæ. The characters of the order are that the species are shrubs or herbs with opposite, or in a few exotic species, alternate, leaves, with or without stipules, generally smelling fragrantly. The petals are usually five in number, broadly spreading, the sepals three, nearly equal, overlapping each other in the bud, with or without two smaller outer ones.

The species figured *H. Vulgare*, is a low under-shrub, with a woody stem; the leaves have stipules; the flowers are of a bright yellow colour, broadly spreading, and blooming from May to September. It is found in dry meadows and pastures throughout Europe and western Asia, and is not uncommon in Great Britain. The Rock Rose, or Cistus of our gardens, is a variety of this species.

SWEET VIOLET.

VIOLA ODORATA.

THE Sweet Violet is a favourite with everybody, and scarcely requires description to be recognized. It is, however, interesting to know that it belongs to the family Violaceæ, and to the only European genus of that family. It has five petals of unequal shape and size, the lower one being drawn out into a kind of spur. There are five sepals, and the stamens are connected together; two of them with curious ear-like appendages. The flowers are of a purplish colour nodding. On the stem we have an example of what are called bracts. The leaves grow at the base of the plant, with rather long stalks, and are broadly heart-shaped. There are several British species of this genus, but our sweet-scented violet, and the pretty blue dog-violet, which is inodorous but very attractive, are those most worthy of notice. Who does not welcome the first violets in the early spring, "gleaming like amethysts in the dewy moss;" and there is no land where these pretty flowers grow in which their praises have not been sung. We must all have felt the power of perfumes in recalling to the memory images and scenes of past years, before these lines were written—

> "The smell of violets hidden in the grass
> Poureth back into my empty soul and frame
> The times when I remember to have been
> Joyful and free from blame." TENNYSON.

Not only is the violet celebrated for its beauty, but for its uses and for its mystic powers. Violet roots and violet flowers have been used as remedies in all sorts of diseases. The Athenians were noted for their love of these flowers, and they were reputed to "moderate anger," to procure sleep, and to comfort and strengthen the heart. At the present time the root is used as an emetic. Pliny prescribes a liniment of violet roots and vinegar for gout and disorders of the spleen. The violet is certainly a classical plant. It was a favourite with the old Greeks. Homer and Virgil both mention it frequently, and Shakespeare alludes to a very old superstition, when he says,—

> "Lay her i' the earth,
> And from her fair and unpolluted flesh
> May violets spring."

HEART'S EASE.

VIOLA TRICOLOR.

THE old English names for this pretty flower are various. It is called in Warwickshire to this time "Love in Idleness," in other places "Pansy," "Kit run the Street," and "Herb Trinity"; but its common name Heart's Ease, from its supposed potency in love charms, seems to us the most appropriate. It belongs to the natural order, Violaceæ, as does its sweet-scented and more modest relative. It is very common in Scotland and the north of England, and although described by botanists as an annual, it is occasionally perennial. The Heart's Ease is considered sacred to St. Valentine, and an old writer says, "while they are fresh and green they are cold and moist under the influence of Venus." We read of the Heart's Ease or

Pansy in 'Shakespeare' on several occasions—poor Ophelia, in her half-crazed love-lorn wanderings, gives away a handful of these pretty flowers, saying,—

"There's Pansies, that's for thoughts."

The wonder-working "little western flower," which so bewitched the Queen of the Fairies in the 'Midsummer Night's Dream,' is thought by critics to be this same Heart's Ease:—

"Yet mark'd I where the bolt of Cupid fell:
It fell upon a little western flower,—
Before milk white, now purple with Love's wound,—
And maidens call it, Love in Idleness.
Fetch me that flower; the herb I showed thee once:
The juice of it on sleeping eyelids laid,
Will make or man or woman madly dote
Upon the next live creature that it sees."

This plant is no exception to the general rule, that in nearly every vegetable product some one has discovered some property which they consider medically valuable. A decoction of it has been recommended to be taken in skin diseases, and poultices made of the leaves are supposed to be efficacious if applied externally. As a cultivated garden plant *Viola Tricolor* is very successful, and is well known. It is one of the few British plants that repays the gardener for cultivation, and is a favourite flower in all exhibitions of horticultural skill

SUNDEW.

DROSERA ROTUNDIFOLIA.

A VERY pretty and curious little plant is the Sundew, or *Drosera Rotundifolia;* and it is found where we should least look for beauty: in bogs and morasses, in the damp corners of heaths and wildernesses, we descry the ruby points of the leaves of this lovely little plant sparkling amid emerald-green moss-tufts. It is the type of the family Droseraceæ, and is now known to be nearly related to the curious plant Dionæa, Venus' Fly-Trap, whose strange meat-eating propensities have lately been fully discussed and described by several naturalists, and have given rise to many interesting and curious experiments at the suggestion of the great original observer, Dr. Darwin. The Drosera has a small flower-stalk, from two to six inches in height, and bears on the top the few little white flowers which expand in the sunshine. The leaves grow very low down, close to the ground, and are of a round shape, and thickly covered with the minute red hairs, each of which secretes a drop of fluid, which sparkles in the sunshine like diamonds. These drops of fluid are of a somewhat glutinous nature, and entrap unwary insects that happen to alight on the leaves. This curious circumstance attracted the notice of naturalists as long ago as the year 1780; but no idea seems to have been

PLATE IV.

SUNDEW. *Drosera rotundifolia.*
LOVE PINK. *Dianthus Caryophyllus.*
FLAX. *Linum usitatissimum.*
GRASS OF PARNASSUS. *Parnassia palustris.*
RED CAMPION. *Lychnis diurna.*
ST. JOHN'S WORT. *Hypericum Calycinum.*

formed as to what became of the insects which were so entrapped until lately. It is now pretty clearly established by a series of experiments, that the Drosera, in common with Dionæa and some other carnivorous plants, capture these insects for the purposes of food, and digest and dissolve them by means of a fluid which is poured out for the purpose, and that they absorb the solution of animal matter so produced. This is probably the only British plant possessing these singular properties; but there are many foreign species in which it exists, and very interesting are the accounts given of them by different observers. The Dionæa crushes its victims to death in its leaves, and covers them over with an acrid juice, by which they are digested. Small bits of meat are absorbed by this plant in the same way if presented to it.

Mr. Canby,* an American botanist, who fed and watched it, says, that when the pieces of beef were completely dissolved the leaf opened again with a dry surface, and ready for another meal, though with an appetite somewhat jaded. He found that cheese disagreed horribly with the leaves, turning them black and finally killing them. He details the useless struggles of an insect to escape; who being of a resolute nature, at last ate his way out of the closed leaf; but was evidently becoming very weak, overcome by the acrid fluid which surrounded him. Then there is

* From an address by Dr. Hooker on Carnivorous Plants before the British Association, 1874.

an American genus of plants called Sarraceina, found chiefly in bogs and shallow water, sending up stalks bearing curiously-shaped flowers with hollow petals, which contain water. These plants, as well as many others, are called Pitcher Plants, and they secrete a sweet and poisonous fluid which tempts and destroys their prey. The flies and insects are attracted by the honey-secreting glands on the edge of the pitcher, and when once within its treacherous cavity, they are unable to get out; are drowned in the water it contains, and made into a sort of broth for the nourishment of the plant. The tropical Pitcher Plants are even more fully developed for a carnivorous diet, and give rise to much speculation, and excite great interest amongst botanists. These examples from a foreign Flora are mentioned in order to call attention to the characteristic family habits of our little British Drosera.

It is somewhat difficult to find the Sundew fully expanded; the best way of seeing it in all its beauty, is to remove a tolerably large portion of the plant with a trowel, and then, placing it in a saucer, surrounded with the damp green moss in which it grows, cover it over with a hand-glass, supply it freely with water, and you have as pretty a little Ward's case as can be imagined, and an interesting subject for botanical study likewise. It is to be found, by careful searching, on Hampstead Heath, on Wimbledon Common, and in most boggy, heathy districts; but since the drainage of these places it is gradually disappearing, and we must go further away from town to find it in any quantity. It has long been known as an acrid and caustic plant, and has been supposed to cause the rot in sheep. It had once a reputation as a cosmetic, and is said to burn away corns and warts. It also curdles milk, and has been frequently used in the dairy for that purpose. This is the plant of which Burton, in his 'Anatomie of Melancholy,' says "that Bernardus Ponottus prefers his herba solis before all the rest of herbs in this disease (melancholy), and will admit of no herb upon the earth to be compared with it." In Italy it is used for making the liquor called Rossoli.

There are other species of Drosera in the British Flora, which possess dyeing properties, as may be seen when they are dried in the herbarium, by the red colour they communicate to the paper.

THE CARNATION, OR CLOVE PINK.

DIANTHUS CARYOPHYLLUS.

This plant is a native of the South of France, but is found wild on old walls in Kent and Norfolk. It belongs to the family Caryophyllaceæ, and is one of a beautiful genus of plants, all of which are sweet-scented and showy. Mr. Babington describes six species of Dianthus as natives of Great Britain. The Clove Pink has solitary flowers; the scales of the calyx are much shorter than the tube of the corolla; the leaves have smooth margins; the petals are toothed, ovate, and smooth; the stem branching, long, and procumbent; the seeds nearly flat, and the flower-stem from twelve to eighteen inches high. The flowers of the genus are of all colours, excepting blue; in the British species they are of a pale pink, and in all cases fragrant. The flowers of the Clove Pink are used to give colour and fragrance to a syrup used in medicine. A small variety of this species is known by the name of Picotees.

THE RED CAMPION.

LYCHNIS DIURNA.

The Red Campion, *Lychnis Diurna*, belongs to the family Caryophyllaceæ. It has oblong leaves, usually pointed, tapering to the base, the lower one stalked. The flowers are few, in loose branches, of a red colour, opening in the morning; the calyx forming a sort of capsule composed of two divisions, or teeth, which curve backwards. The capsule thus formed becomes globular as it ripens. This pretty plant is found in moist shady woods and hedge-banks all over Britain. It flowers all through the summer, beginning early in the spring. The other British species are known by the names of Scarlet Lychnis, Ragged Robin, and

White Campion. The Corn Cockle is also a pretty plant belonging to this family, which is found blossoming in corn-fields from June to September.

FLAX.

LINUM USITATISSIMUM.

ONE of the most valuable of our native plants is the Flax Plant—*Linum Usitatissimum ;* and in the delicate little blue flowers and fragile-looking stem the uninitiated would little imagine the living of thousands and the chief manufacture of a great country to lie concealed. It is a tall, erect annual plant, with alternate narrow-pointed leaves, and flowers of a rich blue colour, arrayed in a loose terminal bunch. The fibre of the plant is woven into linen, and the seeds are valuable on account of the mucilaginous nature of their external coating, and for the oil they contain, which is prized for burning and as a drying medium in the arts ; the oilcake made from the seeds is an extensive article of food for cattle. Flax is chiefly cultivated in Ireland, and from a very early time the importance of its culture was recognized in the economy of this country. In 1750, Sir William Temple wrote a treatise on the subject.

Microscopic examination has clearly proved that the mummy-cloth of Egypt is made of linen fibres, and not, as was once supposed, of cotton. Herodotus and Plutarch tell us that it was not permitted to any Egyptian priest to enter a temple unless he wore a linen garment. By the Greeks, linen was used in the time of Herodotus; possibly not produced by the same species as the one now grown for the purpose, but undoubtedly the fibre of a species of Linum. We have four British species of this genus. None are of any importance but the one we have selected. The Welsh species, or the fairy flax, is an elegant little mountain species, which is remarkable for its beauty and grace, and has a medicinal reputation in its native mountain districts. The exquisite delicacy of the flax plant is aptly pictured by Coleridge :—

> "The unripe flax,
> When through its half-transparent stalk at eve
> The level sunshine glimmers with green light."

THE TREE MALLOW, OR SEA LAVATERA.

LAVATERA ARBOREA.

THE genus Lavatera was named in honour of Lavater (a physician in Zurich, not the celebrated physiognomist of that name), and belongs to the Mallow family—Malvaceæ. The flowers in all the genera of this family are twisted in the bud, the calyx composed of five divisions, with three or more bracts at the base, forming an outer calyx. The species we are now considering has a woody stem, something like that of a cabbage, with thick, hard, flowering branches. The leaves are on long stalks, with seven, five, or three lobes, and soft as velvet. The flowers are mostly in pairs, of a pale purple-red colour, with dark blotches at the base of the petals. It blossoms from July to October, and is found on seaside rocks throughout Europe; in Britain, chiefly on the south and west coasts of England and Ireland, especially in the Isle of Wight, and on the Bass Rock in the Frith of Forth.

THE MUSK MALLOW.

MALVA MOSCHATA.

This plant belongs to the family Malvaceæ. The genus Mallow is a very favourite and well-known group, and most of us may recall, when children, the delight with which we have sought for the plants, in order to secure the much-prized "*cheeses*," or fruits of the mallow. The Musk Mallow has a tough woody root, and an upright partially-branched stem. The root-leaves have long leaf-stalks, with rounded limbs cut into three or five lobes. The stem-leaves are much more deeply cut and lobed than the root-leaves. The whole herbage is more or less hairy. The flowers are large, rose-coloured, or rarely white, crowded together at the top of the stem and branches. The calyx consists of two whorls, the outermost composed of three acute sepals, the innermost five-toothed. The corolla has five wedge-shaped petals jagged at the end. Were this pretty plant less common than it is, it would, perhaps, meet with more admirers; but the extraordinary perverseness of the human mind leads us to admire most that which is least attainable, and to hold an everyday object in slight estimation. The musk-like scent of the particular species of mallow we have selected distinguishes it from the rest, although it be but slight. The Musk Mallow, like the anemone, closes its petals at night. In floral language it is regarded as the emblem of a sweet, mild disposition, and we read that it was customary with the ancients to plant Musk Mallows around the graves of their departed friends. The common mallow, *M. Sylvestris*, yields, when boiled, a plentiful tasteless mucilage, which is used in some cases as a medicine.

MARSH MALLOW.

ALTHÆA OFFICINALIS.

THIS species is also a Malvaceous plant, but belongs to a different genus. Marsh Mallow—*Althæa Officinalis*, is a common European plant, and is often found in marshes, especially near the sea, in great abundance.

PLATE V.

TREE MALLOW. *Lavatera arborea.*
MARSH MALLOW. *Althaea officinalis.*
HERB ROBERT. *Geranium Robertianum.*
MUSK MALLOW. *Malva moschata.*
RED CRANE'S-BILL. *Geranium sang*
WOOD SORRELL. *Oxalis acetosella.*

It is a perennial, with a carrot-shaped, white fleshy root, as thick as the thumb, and a foot or more long. The stems are two or three feet high, covered all over with a soft down, which is also found on the leaves, and gives them a hoary appearance. The leaves are a little heart-shaped and three-lobed. The flowers are not large, of a pale rose colour, and appear in very short clusters from the bosom of the leaves; the calyx is five-toothed, and surrounded with bracts. The whole plant, and particularly the root, abounds in mucilage; the demulcent lozenges sold in the shops under the name of *Pâte de Guimauve*, are made of Marsh Mallow, and a few years ago there was an ointment commonly used, which may still be in repute for aught we know, called Marsh Mallow Ointment. The hollyhock of our gardens is a species of Althæa from the Mediterranean. It is found wild in China.

THE LARGE-FLOWERED HYPERICUM, OR ST. JOHN'S WORT.

HYPERICUM CALYCINUM.

This is a showy plant, belonging to the family Hypericaceæ. It was brought to England by Sir G. Wheeler in 1676, from its native woods near Constantinople. It has been long cultivated in our gardens, and is found wild in bushy places in England and in

Ireland. This species of St. John's Wort has a creeping woody rootstock, the stems scarcely a foot high, simple, and branching at the base only, with large oblong leaves, green and smooth, having very small clear spots on their surface. The flowers are of a bright yellow colour, three or four inches in diameter, with one or two on the top of each stem; in our gardens it is more luxuriant, and produces five or six. There are thirteen British species of this genus, and one hundred and seventy-two are enumerated by De Candolle as growing in various parts of the world. They are all known as St. John's Worts, and most of them are worthy of cultivation. The hardy herbaceous kinds will thrive in any common garden-soil, and are easily propagated by dividing the roots or by seeds. Those which require the greenhouse will thrive best in a mixture of loam and peat, and strike root readily under a hand-glass.

The *Hypericum Perforatum*, the perforated St. John's Wort, was one of the flowers gathered by our forefathers to be thrown into the bonfires which were kindled in London on the eve of St. John. In many parts of France and Germany the peasants still gather its golden blossoms, and hang them with much ceremony in their windows and doorways, as a charm against evil spirits, storms, thunder, and all calamities. This custom probably arose from the misinterpretation of some medical writers, who, believing in its virtue as a remedy in maniacal disorders, called it *Fuga*

Dæmonum. It was at one time worn about the person in Scotland as a protection against witchcraft and enchantment.

GRASS OF PARNASSUS.

PARNASSIA PALUSTRIS.

HERE we are among the gods; but surely this pretty plant has mistaken its habitation, for we find it in marshy, boggy places, and scarcely ever on elevated land. The Grass of Parnassus, or *Parnassia Palustris,* belongs to the same family of plants as our little Sundew—*Droseraceæ;* and it is often found in the same localities. Why it is called a grass we cannot imagine; for with its delicately-coloured flowers beautifully netted, it does not resemble the family of grasses at all. The leaves around the roots are on long stalks, while here and there a leaf clasps the flower-stem. Each flower-stalk produces but one flower, which has curious fringed scales, which lie around the centre, and are the nectaries; a little wax-like gland exists at the tip of each hair. In former times, this flower was called the Noble Liverwort, and was doubtless considered a remedy in diseases of the liver. It is the only British species of the genus. Sir William Hooker tells us that this elegant plant, if plunged into water in a garden-pot, surrounded by a ball of its native earth, will continue to blossom for many weeks.

RED CRANE'S-BILL, OR THE BLOOD GERANIUM.
GERANIUM SANGUINEUM.

THE Blood Geranium grows in great profusion on our western limestone coasts, and is one of the most attractive of the species. The family to which it belongs is Geraniaceæ; of which the characters are well preserved in the genus Geranium.

The plants known by this name must not be confounded with the so-called geraniums of our gardens, which, though of the order Geraniaceæ, belong to the subdivision *Pelargonium*. The five petals of our true geranium are of the same size, while the inferior petals of the pelargoniums are smaller than the other two, and of a different character.

Geranium Sanguineum is known by its numerous stems, about a foot long, leaning downwards, or sometimes upright, with spreading hairs. The peduncles are mostly single-flowered; the carpels smooth, crowned with a few bristles; the leaves nearly round, seven-lobed. The flowers are large, of a dark purple colour; the sepals hairy, with a fine point. The whole plant somewhat resembles the mallow in appearance, and there is an Eastern notion that geraniums were at first simply mallows, until Mahommed, delighted with the fine texture of a shirt made for him of mallow fibres, turned that plant into the more beautiful geranium; or some assert that his shirt being spread to dry on a mallow plant, the transformation was discovered on taking it up. There are above a dozen British geraniums; the most common one, probably, being *G. Robertianum*, the Herb Robert. The root of *G. Maculatum*, or Alum-root, is a really powerful astringent, containing more tannin than catechu or kino. In North America it is employed as a remedy in sore throat among children. The beautiful red colour assumed by the leaves in dyeing may have been suggestive of their efficacy in arresting hæmorrhages; the fancy is scarcely more absurd than our modern doctrine "that like cures like."

HERB ROBERT.

GERANIUM ROBERTIANUM.

THIS pretty plant is also one of the Crane's-bills, and belongs to the family Geraniaceæ. It is one of the earliest to appear on the sunny banks in the spring-time with blue-bells and primroses, and lasts long into the summer, when, by the presence of more attractive blossoms, it is often overlooked. All lovers of wild flowers know the Herb Robert and recognize its small clumps of leaves cut into numerous segments, looking beautiful by their redness, which tint deepens in autumn to a glowing crimson. In common with its family it has a very disagreeable odour. The common name is said by Dr. Withering to have been given to it after a celebrated curator in the Botanic Garden at Oxford; but more probably it originated in its being used in Germany to cure a disease called "Ruprecht's Plage," in allusion to Robert Duke of Normandy, for whom the celebrated work of the Middle Ages, 'Ortus Sanitatis,' was written. The name occurs in a MS. vocabulary of the thirteenth century.

According to the old doctrine of signatures the red colour of the leaves indicates its value in staunching blood, for which purpose our much-believing friend, Old Gerarde, greatly extols it. In Wales it is still administered in medicine.

Herb Robert is a very common plant on the shingly beach of the south and east of England, and very pretty it looks with its tiny bright flowers and curious long beak which terminates the carpels.

THE WOOD SORREL.
OXALIS ACETOSELLA.

The Wood Sorrel, *Oxalis Acetosella*, belongs to the same family as the Geranium—Geraniaceæ. It is easily recognized by its three delicately green leaflets, with longish stalks, marked with a darkish crescent in the centre, veined, and its lovely white flowers, which at first sight resemble the wood anemone. There are few walks or shady woods where, in the early spring, the bright half-folded green leaves of this pretty little plant may not be found. The tiny white flowers, with their delicate purple veins, are called by the Welsh "fairy bells," and are believed to ring the merry peals which call the elves to "Moonlight dance and revelry." The whole plant abounds in an acid cooling juice, which contains oxalic acid. An infusion of the leaves is frequently administered as a cooling drink in Russia, and the salt prepared from it is used under the name of "salt of sorrel," to remove the stains of ink and iron-mould from linen. Among the Druids, its triple leaflets were regarded as a mysterious symbol of a trinity, the full meaning of which was involved in darkness. So, too, St. Patrick chose this leaf as his symbol to illustrate the doctrine he sought to teach, and converted many by the apt use of an illustration derived from a plant already sacred in the eyes of his hearers. The original *shamrock* was undoubtedly the Oxalis; though the name became applied to all sorts of trefoiled plants. In all ages, the trefoiled leaf has been regarded with veneration, especially when, departing from its usual form, it is found with four leaflets. The old song, "I'll seek a four-leaved Shamrock," tells of the fairy spells to be woven with its enchantment.

The wood sorrel approaches nearest of all our native plants to a sensitive plant, not only closing its petals and folding its bright green leaves at sunset, and with every change of atmosphere, but even if the stem be rudely or repeatedly struck. In a flower-saucer, or pan covered with a glass shade, this pretty plant forms a lovely object; and we have frequently seen it blossoming year after year in a Ward's case or under a hand-glass, covering the space given to it with its delicate white blossoms. An old Welsh proverb says—

> "Three things let no one trust such as shall dislike them,—
> The scent of trefoils, the taste of milk, the song of birds."

GORSE, FURZE, OR HULM.

ULEX EUROPÆUS.

THIS plant must not be confounded with the Broom, which belongs also to the natural order Leguminosæ, and is not unlike it in general appearance. Both plants also have bright yellow flowers; but the Gorse abounds in spines or prickles, as all must find out who attempt to gather its showy blossoms or to regale themselves with its delicious perfume. Although so common on almost every heath and waste piece of land it is not a very hardy plant, and severe frosts sometimes kill it and often bite it down to the ground; but it shoots up again in the spring. Linnæus is said to have lamented that he could not keep it alive in Sweden even in a green-house. It was one of his favourite plants, and it is related that, when he first saw it in flower on Hounslow Heath he fell on his knees and thanked God for having created so beautiful a plant. The same story is told of Dillenius, so we may doubt its authenticity. The common name of Furze-bush or Furze given to the Gorse is of obscure origin; some say it is derived from fir, being like these coniferous firs used for firewood or fuel; but it seems more likely that it was suggested by the bright yellow flame-like flowers which appear almost like a "fire" or "Furze" bush. Before the days of Linnæus the Gorse and the Broom were classed together both as Brooms, and it was called *Genista Spinosa;* but Linnæus restored to it the name of Ulex, by which it has ever since been recognized. In France the Gorse is used commonly as fuel, and is cut down every few years for the purpose. Even in some parts of England it is largely used to heat ovens, and cultivated with that object. In the county of Surrey it is grown and cut down every three years simply as fuel for the bakers.

The young shoots are eaten by cattle, and even the older branches, when put into a mill and crushed, are given to horses and cows to eat; but we can hardly divest ourselves of the notion that the chief value of this beautiful plant is its picturesque beauty, and, although it is curious to trace the uses of any plant from an economic point of view, the pleasure felt at the sight of a mass of the golden yellow blossoms of the Furze brightening the heath and open lands as they do in May and June, must be sufficient to give it a claim to our attention. There is no season of the year that there are not blossoms on the Gorse: hence the old proverb—that "When Gorse is out of bloom kissing is out of season;" but it is in the spring time when its golden blossoms are most abundant, and when its delicious cocoa-nut-like perfume "comes wafting o'er the breeze."

In Wickliffe's translation of the Bible we read in Isaiah:—"A fir tre schal stre for a gorst, and myrte tre schal waxe for a netal."

In calm and sunny weather the crackling caused by the bursting of the seed pods of the Furze bushes is often very audible.

> "The path with laughing Furze o'errun,
> When bursting seed bells crackle in the sun."

We may be sure that English poets have never been insensible to the charms of this beautiful native, and many lines occur to us which sing its praises.

> "The Furze, in russet frock arrayed
> With saffron knots, like shepherd maid,
> Broadly tricked out her rough brocade;
> The singèd mosses curling here,—
> A golden fleece too short to shear,—
> Crumbled to sparkling dust beneath
> My light step on that summer heath

Old Gerarde, writing in the time of Queen Elizabeth, says, that he was requested by " divers earnest letters " to send this shrub to Dantzic and Poland, where the plants "are most curiously kept in their fairest gardens." We agree with our old-fashioned poet Cowper, who, in recommending a walk, suggests—

> "The common, overgrown with fern, and rough
> With prickly Gorse—that, shapeless and deformed
> And dangerous to the touch, has yet its bloom,
> And decks itself with ornaments of gold,—
> Yields no unpleasing ramble."

THE REST HARROW.

ONONIS SPINOSA.

THIS plant belongs to the Pea-flower family, or Leguminosæ. It is a low spreading little shrub, with hard, tough, trailing roots, which often retard the progress of the plough, while its numerous and thorny branches are so great an impediment to the action of the harrow in turning up the ground, as to have obtained for it the common English name of Rest-

Harrow. Frequently the whole plant is clothed with sharp hairs or prickles, but sometimes they are quite soft, and the plant smooth, according to the soil in which it grows. The leaflets are oblong or obovate. The flowers are solitary, on short branches of a pink colour, sometimes streaked with a darker shade. It is often very abundant on the sandy cliffs near the seashore. This little plant has its uses; for although in its thorny state no animal but the donkey will eat it, yet on better soils it mingles with the pasture, and is relished by cows, sheep, and goats. The roots are succulent and sweet, and have been considered good as a pickle. In the time of Queen Elizabeth they were often brought to table in this form.

THE STRAWBERRY CLOVER.

TRIFOLIUM FRAGIFERUM.

EVERY ONE must have noticed, and perhaps gathered, this plant, wondering whether it were fruit or flower, scarcely recognizing in the tiny red heads, the closely-packed flowers surrounded by an involucre of bracts. It belongs to the family Leguminosæ, and is found chiefly in damp meadows and in moist places near the sea In the neighbourhood of London it is not uncommon. There are many British species of clover. Mr. Babington describes twenty-one. The white or

PLATE VI.

:ST HARROW. *Ononis Spinosa.* STRAWBERRY CLOVER. *Trifolium,*
:LLOW VETCHLING. *Lathyrus aphaca.* GORSE. *Ulex Europaeus.*
ILLOW HERB. *Epilobium angustifolium.* EVENING PRIMROSE. *Oenothera bi*

Dutch clover is very largely cultivated, and is now often used as the representative of the true shamrock, or three-leaved plant of Ireland. The original mystic plant was doubtless the Oxalis, of which we have before spoken. Leaves of this character have from a very remote period been regarded with superstitious veneration.

"The holy trefoil's charm"

was considered potent against all manner of evil.

COMMON DOG ROSE.

ROSA CANINA.

BOOKS have been written on Roses alone, and when we think of the numbers of varieties of this beautiful plant, and remember that they all originally sprang from the simple rose of our hedges, we feel especially drawn to it as the progenitor of so much delicious beauty. All roses belong to the natural order Rosaceæ, and there are but few people who are ignorant enough to mistake a rose, whether wild or cultivated, for any other flower. Its very scent is more fragrant and distinctive than that of any other flower, and the soft velvety texture of its petals, its delicate and varied hues, all combine to make it the Queen of Flowers. Even the modest little hedge-rose, so great a favourite with children, and with all who have the simple, unspoiled taste of childhood, has a beauty of its own. It sits amidst its pretty dark compact green leaves like a princess, and appears to look down at the little flowers struggling on the bank beneath, and at the climbing honeysuckle and bryony which twine around its branches, and seem as though they wished to pay court to its beauty. In exhaustive works on Botany we find more than a dozen varieties of our common Dog Rose, and it requires some knowledge to be able to distinguish them—for their differences are small, though important to the botanist. We can never gather a wild rose and admire its pretty tinted pink buds and lovely fragile full-blown petals, surrounding its cluster of yellow stamens, without thinking of the more gorgeous relations it boasts of in our gardens, natives and inhabitants of other and warmer climes. The China rose, native of the Celestial Empire, and growing there in wild profusion, varies from a delicate blush colour to a deep crimson. It abounds in the neighbourhood of Canton, and blossoms six or eight times a year. In the south of France it flourishes well out of doors; but does not well bear the climate of England, though a hybrid variety is well known in our gardens as the tea-scented China rose.

The fruit of the rose, whether wild or cultivated, is well known, and in the country hedges "hips," as they are called, are very popular as material for making a homely conserve with sugar. It is an article which is also included in the British Pharmacopœia. Although these pretty red berries are called fruits they are not so in reality, but are the enlarged persistent calyx enclosing the real fruits, which are very numerous, and are clothed, as well as the inside of the calyx, with silky hairs. In preparing them for medicinal use these hairs are carefully removed and the fleshy calyx beaten to a pulp, to which is gradually added three times its weight of sugar. It is used by druggists as a vehicle for other medicines, and is a very pleasant and wholesome preparation in itself. In former times, when garden fruit was scarce and not imported cheaply from other countries, "hips" were thought good enough for dessert, and Gerarde assures us that the hips of the rose maketh the most pleasant meats and banqueting dishes, and tarts, and such like, the making whereof "he commits to the cunning cooke, and teethe to eate them in the riche man's mouthe." The petals of roses form a delicate dish at Chinese banquets, and we read of a *ragôut* of the flowers of the common China rose dressed whole and served at a feast at Shanghae. Such things are not unknown here, indeed, for amidst the numberless delicate preparations of sugared bonbons we have but lately seen dishes of tinted rose-leaves preserved in sugar.

The rose has ever been a favourite flower with poets and amongst Oriental writers. We are told in Eastern story that it is the chosen flower of the melodious nightingale, amongst the branches of which he sits and sings out his love tale, and the delicate petals of which constitute his only food.

> "For there the rose o'er crag and vale,—
> Sultana to the nightingale,—
> Blooms blushing to her lover's tale,
> His queen, his garden queen, his rose."

The scent of the rose, delicious as it is here, never attains the perfect fragrance and power that it does in hotter countries, where it is cultivated solely for the purpose of extracting its perfume. Its costliness is considerable, as we know from the high price and difficulty of obtaining a drop of genuine attar of roses.

Englishmen glory in the rose as their national emblem, for ever happily blended with the thistle and the shamrock; but it is not to be forgotten that at one time it was the symbol of national war and bloodshed, when the Red and the White Roses, and those that wore them, as nearly related to each other as the flowers themselves, waged a deadly fight with each other; when, according to Shakespeare, Warwick says to Plantagenet—

> "——This brawl to-day,
> Grown to this faction, in the Temple Garden,
> Shall send, between the Red Rose and the White,
> A thousand souls to death and deadly night."

An old author penned the following lines, worthy of Anacreon, on presenting a white rose to a Lancastrian lady:—

PLATE VII.

LE LOOSE-STRIFE. *Lythrum salicaria.* CREEPING CINQUEFOIL. *Potentilla rep*
ROSE. *Rosa canina.* BURNET ROSE. *Rosa Spinosissima.*
BRYONY. *Bryonia Dioica.* HOUSE LEEK. *Sempervivum tectorum.*

> "If this fair rose offend thy sight
> It in thy bosom wear,
> 'Twill blush to find itself less white,
> And turn Lancastrian there."

We could write a volume on the poems, legends, and fancies connected with the rose, with which indeed the name of England has been associated ages before the brawl in the Temple Gardens. The elder Pliny, in discussing the origin of the word Albion, suggests that the land may have been so called from the number of white roses which grew in it. Whatever we may think of the etymology of this old Roman, we can at least indulge in fancies as to the reports given by the invaders but lately returned from Britain, as to the woods and flowery hedge-rows under which they had often rested during their sojourn in our island. And we look with almost a new pleasure on our own wild roses when we regard them as direct descendants of the "rosas alba" of those far-off summers.

The pink Dog Rose used to be called the *Canker*, a name it still retains in some parts of the country; but which we consider a libel on our pretty rose. Hotspur alludes to this in Shakespeare's play, when he accuses the Earls of Northumberland and Worcester of trying

> "To put down Richard, that sweet lovely rose,
> And plant this thorn, this canker, Bolingbroke!"

thereby meaning a usurper, which is certainly an unfair term as applied to our own native wild hedge-side rose, blooming in our quiet country lanes, perfuming the air and charming all passers by with its simple beauty.

COMMON BURNET ROSE.

ROSA SPINOSISSIMA.

ANY ONE who has been attracted by the pretty flowers of this little rose, on its tiny low bush in the midst of a sandy waste near the sea-shore, which is its favourite abode, and has attempted recklessly to gather the tempting sprays, will understand the signification of its specific name; for no rose ever seemed to us so spiny or so sharp. It has the prettiest little leaves, and grows in daintily-formed sprays, which appear quite easy to pluck until we try. It is also known as the Scotch rose, and is said to be the parent of the Ayrshire rose of our gardens, and of all our pretty Scotch roses. It is seldom met with inland, and grows chiefly on sandy downs near the sea, both in the north and south of England. I found it in profusion in Cumberland. This was the rose found by Sir W. Hooker in Iceland.

THE YELLOW VETCHLING, OR YELLOW PEA.

LATHYRUS APHACA.

THIS plant is a common European field plant, belonging to the natural order Leguminosæ. It is a little smooth pale-green annual, branching from the root into several weak stems, either lying on the ground or climbing by means of numerous alternate simple tendrils, each of which springs from between a pair of large stipules of a broad arrow-shape. There are no true leaves or leaflets, except now and then near the root. The flowers are solitary on simple stalks, small, drooping, and lemon-coloured. The bracts are in pairs, oval-shaped; the teeth of the calyx long and lanceolate, ribbed. The pod is about an inch in length, smooth, and containing about six round seeds, which are somewhat narcotic, and produce excessive headache if eaten abundantly when ripe. In their young and green state they may be eaten like green peas without inconvenience. *L. Sylvestris*, the everlasting pea, is a well-known and pretty species of the same genus. It is cultivated in our gardens, and is often found wild in England. The genus *Lathyrus* is nearly allied to *Vicia*, the true vetches, of which there are many very pretty British species; *Vicia Cracca*, the tufted or purple vetch, is one of the most attractive. We can imagine that it must have been this pretty flower which suggested to Sir Walter Scott these lines :—

> "And where profuse the wood-vetch clings
> Round ash and elm in verdant rings,
> Its pale and azure pencill'd flower
> Should canopy Titania's bower."

CREEPING CINQUEFOIL.

POTENTILLA REPTANS.

THIS is a common British plant, belonging to the family Rosaceæ, and is found on heaths, moors, and open pastures throughout Europe. The stems are prostrate, and creep along the ground, rooting at the joints for a considerable distance. The stipules are ovate, and mostly entire; the calyx hairy. The leaves are stalked with five obovate or oblong coarsely-toothed leaflets. The petals are large, of a bright yellow colour, mostly five in number, sometimes four. This pretty plant is found on the borders of meadows, edges of woods, and hedges throughout Europe and Asia. It greatly resembles the common *Tormentilla*, and is often mistaken for it. The latter is an astringent plant, and has been used medicinally; also for tanning in the Western Islands of Scotland and the Orkneys.

WILLOW-HERB, OR CODLINS AND CREAM.

EPILOBIUM ANGUSTIFOLIUM.

APPLE-PIE PLANT, as it is called, is a very handsome plant, belonging to the family Onagraciæ. It has a creeping root, an erect, nearly simple, stem, slightly hoary, but not hairy, like another species, *E. Nilobium Hirsutum.* The leaves are shortly stalked, lanceolate, entire, or with very minute distinct teeth. The flowers are large, purplish red, in long bunches; the petals are slightly unequal, entire, and spreading from the base; the stamens and styles inclined downwards. The stigmas are deeply four-lobed. The pod is from one to two inches long, more or less hoary. It is found in mountains, woods, and meadows, in Europe and Siberia. In Great Britain it is found in moist places in the north of England, and in the south of Scotland. It has crimson, inodorous flowers, with blue pollen. It is a showy plant, and is often transplanted into gardens, where, however, it must be carefully watched, or its creeping roots will encroach on other plants. The down of the seeds furnishes that soft downy substance which, either alone or mixed with cotton, is often woven into stockings, gloves, and such things. The leaves are used in the adulteration of tea, or as a substitute for it. Its young root-stalks and suckers are boiled and eaten; and the Kamtschatkans make a beer from an infusion of the plant. The pith is dried and boiled, and on being fermented is converted into vinegar.

The name willow-herb is given probably from some slight resemblance in the outline of the leaves to those of a species of willow; and perhaps, too, the situations in which the greater part of the species grow being near the water, or in it, may account for it.

Gerarde says the willow-herbs stop bleeding, heal wounds, and drive away snakes, gnats, and flies.

THE EVENING PRIMROSE, OR COMMON ŒNOTHERA.

ŒNOTHERA BIENNIS.

ŒNOTHERA BIENNIS belongs to the same family as the willow-herb—Onagraciæ. It is a biennial, with ovate, lanceolate, flat, toothed leaves, a rough hairy stem; the petals longer than the stamens, and about half as long as the tube of the calyx. The flowers are large, numerous, and of a bright yellow colour, emitting a slight fragrance. They close in the bright daylight, and open themselves as the sun goes down: hence their name. It is found abundantly on the Lancashire coast, and covers several acres of ground near Woodbridge in Suffolk. The Suffolk poet Bernard Barton has immortalized this, his native flower, in some beautiful lines, which we cannot refrain from quoting here :—

> "Fair flower that shunn'st the glare of day,
>   Yet lov'st to open, meekly bold,
> To evening's hues of sober grey,
>   Thy cup of paly gold.
>
> I love to watch, at silent eve,
>   Thy scatter'd blossoms' lonely light,
> And have my inmost heart receive
>   The influence of that sight.
>
> I love at such an hour to mark
>   Their beauty greet the night-breeze chill,
> And shine 'mid shadows gathering dark
>   The garden's glory still.
>
> For such 'tis sweet to think awhile,
>   When cares and griefs the breast invade ;
> In friendship's animating smile,
>   In sorrow's dark'ning shade.
>
> Thus it bursts forth like thy pale cup,
>   Glistening amid its dewy tears,
> And bears the sinking spirit up
>   Amid its chilling fears.
>
> But still more animating far,
>   If meek religion's eye may trace,
> E'en in thy glimmering earth-born star
>   The holier hopes of grace.
>
> The hope,—that as thy beauteous bloom
>   Expands to glad the close of day,
> So through the shadows of the tomb
>   May break forth mercy's ray."

The pretty plant which suggested to the mind of our Quaker poet these beautiful thoughts is the only native species. It is sometimes called the Tree

Primrose. The roots are eatable, and were formerly taken after dinner to flavour wine, as olives now are; therefore, the genuine name was changed from *Onagra*, the Ass Food, to *Œnothera*, the Wine-trap. We are not sure whether the change was necessary for such as need an incentive to imprudent potations.

PURPLE LOOSE-STRIFE.

LYTHRUM SALICARIA.

THIS is a showy plant belonging to the family Lythraceæ. It has a perennial root-stock, with short annual erect stems, two or three feet high, slightly branched, glabrous, or softly downy. The leaves are of a dark-green colour, opposite, or sometimes in threes, sessile, clasping the stem at the base, lanceolate and entire, from two to three inches long. The flowers are of a reddish-purple or pink colour, in whorled, leafy spikes. It is the *Lysimachia* of Pliny, a name which is applied to the Yellow Loose-Strife of our hedges. Our word Loose-Strife is a simple translation of this Latin word. A strong decoction of this plant acts as an astringent, as it contains tannic acid.

WILD BRYONY, OR RED BRYONY.

BRYONIA DIOICA.

A PLANT belonging to the Cucumber family—Cucurbitaceæ, must not be confounded with the Black Bryony, *Tamus Communis*, which is a very different plant, and about which we shall hear presently. It has a thick, tuberous, perennial root-stock, sometimes branched, the annual stems climbing to a great length; it is rough with minute hairs, containing an acrid juice, and emitting a sickly smell when drying. The tendrils are simple or branched, and spirally twisted. The leaves are divided into five or seven coarsely-toothed lobes, of which the middle is the largest. The barren and fruitful flowers are on the same plant, but on different stalks. The barren flowers are placed in small bunches, several together, and are of a pale yellow colour; the fruitful flowers are much smaller, generally two together, nearly round. The berries are red or orange, about four lines in diameter, containing several flat seeds.

It is a very common plant in hedges and thickets in England, but it is not found in Scotland and Ireland.

HOUSE LEEK.

SEMPERVIVUM TECTORUM.

HOUSE LEEK, *Sempervivum Tectorum;* so named from its tenacity of life; from *semper* and *vivo*, always living. The little plant known by this name belongs to the family Crassulaceæ. There is but one British species. The foreign varieties are some of them very elegant, and are grown in gardens and greenhouses. Our own species was originally a native of the Alpine and sub-Alpine regions of Central Europe, but it has now found its way to the tops of old walls, and the thatched and tiled roofs of the houses of all the countries of Europe. It is frequently called Jupiter's Eye, Bullock's Eye, or Jupiter's Beard. It has very thick and fleshy leaves, the lower ones, one to one inch and a half long, ending in a small point, and bordered by a line of short stiff hairs. The flowers are pink, arranged along the spreading branches of the cyme, without stalks. The petals are twelve in number, smooth within, fringed with delicate hairs at the edges and on the outside.

This plant is very closely associated with the Stonecrops or Sedums, and shares with them virtues both supernatural and physical. It is considered lucky by the Welsh peasantry to have their roofs covered with these plants; they are believed to protect the house from the ravages of the elements, and to ensure the prosperity of the inmates. Pliny mentions the stonecrop as infallible for procuring sleep; but to produce this effect the plant must be wrapped in black cloth, and carefully introduced under the pillow of the patient without his knowledge. The juice of the House Leek, when mixed with cream or applied by itself, is said to give relief in burns and other external inflammations. Its vitality is such, that it survives the longest droughts, and the rapidity with which it reproduces itself, even after the roughest treatment, is surprising. Its power of continuing to live under the most adverse circumstance is owing to the facility with which it abstracts carbonic acid gas from the atmosphere. This substance is the food of all plants, and it is thus that they take out of the air and appropriate to their own nourishment what would be injurious to man.

THE MARSH SAXIFRAGE.

SAXIFRAGA HIRCULUS.

THE Saxifrages are called also Stone-breaks, from the wonderful manner in which the fibres of their roots penetrate the strongest rocks and most unpromising soils. The genus *Saxifraga* is the type of the family Saxifragaceæ. Our example is the Yellow Marsh Saxifrage. The stem is solitary, from four to eight inches long, sometimes covered with rusty hairs. The stem has a purplish hue, and bears but one rather large yellow flower with red dots. The leaves are alternate, narrow, oblong or linear, and entire. This is one of the rare plants which it is so interesting to find. It inhabits wet, turfy moors, at high elevations, and has not yet been supposed to extend further north than Berwick. It is worth cultivation, and will grow well in peaty bog earth. The saxifrages of Great Britain include the London Pride, that pretty well-known flower of the gardens, which is the *S. Umbrosa*.

The *S. Oppositifolia*, or Purple Saxifrage, is a favourite spring plant, which, though found growing in wild luxuriance on Welsh and Highland mountains, is eagerly sought for and sold in Covent Garden Market as an early spring flower. There are many other British species. Mr. Bentham describes thirteen. Medicinal properties have been attributed to some of them, and the white flowers of the common saxifrage were supposed to indicate that it was "governed by the moon."

THE WATER PARSNIP.

SIUM ANGUSTIFOLIUM.

THE narrow-leaved Water Parsnip is a plant belonging to the family Umbelliferæ. It has an erect stem, branched and leafy. The leaves pinnate, the leaflets unequally lobed and serrated; the umbels or branch of flowerets, opposite the leaves. It is found in wet ditches and shallow streams, and being of a poisonous nature, ought to be carefully distinguished from the water-cress, with which it often grows. Another species, *S. Nodiflorum*, is, however, more frequently mistaken, and is therefore called Fool's Water-cress.

THE GOLDEN SAXIFRAGE.

CHRYSOPLENIUM ALTERNIFOLIUM.

This plant belongs to the order Saxifragaceæ, but is not certainly a true Saxifrage. The habit of thus giving common English names to plants of different genera leads to much confusion. It has alternate leaves, the lower ones kidney-shaped, hairy, and seated on long stalks. The flowers are small, in little branches surrounded by leaves, and of a deep yellow colour. It is not a common plant in Great Britain, although pretty generally distributed. It flowers in the spring by the sides of rivulets, and in moist shady places.

MARSH PENNYWORT.

HYDROCOTYLE VULGARIS.

An Umbelliferous plant, having a slender perennial stem, creeping along the wet mud, or even floating in water; rooting at every joint, and sending out from the same point small tufts of leaves and flowers. The leaves are orbicular, one to one inch and a half in diameter, smooth, and attached by the centre to rather a long stalk. The flowers are very small, white, and on short stalks. The shape and size of these leaves somewhat resemble a piece of money; hence the name pennywort. It is also known as Pennygrass, White-rot, Fluke-wort, and Sheep's-bane. These latter names it has obtained on account of its being supposed to produce the rot and other diseases in animals that feed upon it. This is, however, an error, as it does not produce disease, but occurs in damp, moist situations, where animals that feed are likely to be attacked with rot and other diseases.

SEA HOLLY.

ERYNGIUM MARITIMUM.

I am glad to write again of a sea-shore plant, for I associate with them quiet bright holiday hours; the never-weary sea, rippling on the clean smooth

PLATE VIII.

MARSH SAXIFRAGE. *Saxifraga Hirculus.* GOLDEN SAXIFRAGE. {*Chysoplenium Alternifolium.*}
WATER PARSNIP. *Sium Angustifolium.* MARSH PENNYWORT. *Hydrocotyle Vulgaris.*
SEA HOLLY. *Eryngium Maritimum.* SAMPHIRE. *Crithmum Maritimum.*

beach; happy children with spades and willing hands, making fairy gardens in the sand, filled with the wild flowers which grow around and up the sides of the cliffs, whither they climb, regardless of downfalls, to secure their treasures; but woe to the little hands that recklessly seize in their grasp the treacherous Sea Holly, with its stiff, sharp-pointed, prickly leaves! They are covered with a bluish or sea-green bloom, being what is called in botany, glaucous. This character is very common in plants growing near the sea, but not confined to them. One would not easily recognize the Eryngium as an Umbelliferous plant; but if it is carefully examined, it will be found to preserve all the characteristics of the order. The upper leaves embrace the stem, which is about a foot high, and are lobed and palmate in shape. The flowers are in heads rather than umbels, of a pale blue colour. It is very abundant on the eastern shores of England, and is found in Scotland and Ireland. The plant is often called Sea Eryngo, Sea Hulver, and Sea Holme. According to Linnæus, the flower-shoots are very good when boiled and eaten like asparagus. The leaves are sweetish, with a warm aromatic flavour. The root also is sweet to the taste, and has a warm, aromatic smell. It has been used in medicine, and was recommended by Boerhaave, the great Danish physician. It is candied and sold in the shops in London as a sweet-meat. At Colchester, in Essex, there exists an establishment where this

F

preparation was first made, more than two centuries ago, by Robert Buxton, an apothecary. There is also another British species, *E. Campestre*, called by John Ray Friar's Goose.

THE SAMPHIRE.

CRITHMUM MARITIMUM.

The Samphire is also an Umbelliferous plant. Those who have once seen it and smelt it will recognize it again. It grows in places where none but the adventurous can reach—on the sides of cliffs, near the sea, and in the clefts of rocks; it fringes the edges of precipices with its bright-green succulent leaves and tiny blossoms. It is almost woody at the base; the young branches, foliage, and umbels, thick and fleshy. The leaves are twice or thrice ternate, with thick linear segments about an inch long. The flowers are greenish, or yellowish-white, in umbels of fifteen to twenty or more rays. The samphire is warm and aromatic in flavour, and is frequently used as a pickle. Visitors to the sea-side, who wish to try this pleasant condiment, cannot do better than look for it on the sides of the cliffs, and, if within reach, gather a basketful of its bright green leaves; they should be separated from the stalks and flowers, and then have spice and boiled vinegar poured on them in the usual way. Samphire-gathering, when pursued as a trade, frequently leads to loss of life, and terrible dangers are encountered to secure it. It has almost a classical association, since Shakespeare immortalized it in 'King Lear.' It grows well on chalk rocks, such as form the cliffs at Dover; there, Edgar is supposed to be leading Gloucester along, and says—

> "Come on, sir; here's the place: stand still. How fearful
> And dizzy 'tis, to cast one's eyes so low!
> The crows and choughs, that wing the midway air,
> Show scarce so gross as beetles. Halfway down
> Hangs one that gathers samphire; dreadful trade!
> Methinks he seems no bigger than his head:
> The fishermen that walk upon the beach
> Appear like mice."

It abounds also in the Isle of Wight and many other sea-coasts of England, especially in the south, where, with its bright green colour, it gives quite a character to the cliffs and caves which overhang the sea.

GOOSE-GRASS.

GALIUM ASSARINE.

THIS troublesome little plant, which is always catching one's dress and clinging to everything it touches, must be familiar to all who enjoy country walks. It belongs to the natural order Rubiaceæ, and is familiarly called Cleavers, Catch-weed, and Scratch-weed. The name Goose-Grass it derives from the fact of its being a favourite food of these birds, and when they are turned out into the fields or on the commons just before Michaelmas one may often see them busily devouring it. In old herbals we find the Goose-Grass supposed to be endorsed with wonderful medicinal powers, and our old friend Gerarde writes of it as a marvellous remedy for the bites of snakes, spiders, and all venomous creatures. He also quotes Pliny as an authority for the statement, that a pottage made of "Cleavers, a little mutton and oatmeal," is good "to cause lanknesse and keepe from fatnesse." This presumption would hardly recommend itself to modern believers in Banting. According to Linnæus the stalks are used in Sweden as a filter to strain milk through. Dioscorides relates that the shepherds made the same use of it in his time. It is considered even now in rural districts to be a purifier of the blood, and for that purpose the tops are often put into spring broth. It appears, however, that very many of our wayside herbs are valuable in diet on account of the salts which they contain; but most of them are overlooked and despised in favour of more costly and cultivated herbs.

MISTLETOE.

VISCUM ALBUM.

OUR next plant is associated with thoughts of pleasant meetings and festive boards, and happy are those whose homes are filled at Christmas time with the cheerful companions of summer rambles, having health and spirits to enjoy the good gifts of God in any form. The Mistletoe, or *Viscum Album*, is one of a genus of parasitical plants belonging to the family Loranthaceæ, and is the only British representative of the family.

"Mistletoe," says Lord Bacon, "chiefly grows on crab-trees, apple-trees, sometimes upon hazels, and rarely upon oaks, the Mistletoe whereof is accounted very medicinal. It is an evergreen that bears a white glittering berry, and differs entirely from the tree whereon it grows. It continues green winter and summer, which the tree does not."

> "Nought was green upon the oak,
> But moss and rarest mistletoe."

In many respects the Mistletoe is an object of great interest to the naturalist. The manner in which it derives its nourishment from other plants by engrafting itself into the branches of a tree, and the curious conditions of the seeds in germination, are worthy of attention.

I need scarcely describe the plant so familiar to us

all, as there is little fear of its being mistaken for any other. I may, however, say that the leaves are entire, varying from narrow oblong to nearly oval—thick, fleshy, and always obtuse. There are two kinds of flowers, those bearing pistils and those bearing stamens, each on separate plants: they are very small, and are placed in little heads, about three to five in each. The berry is about the size, and has somewhat the appearance, of a white currant, very smooth, viscid, and containing a simple seed. The manner in which the plant establishes itself in the branch of a tree has been much discussed. Old botanists believed that the "Mistletoe Thrush" feeding upon the berries surrounded his beak with the viscid mucus they contain, and in order to get rid of it, rubbed his beak against the branches, and thus inserted the seeds, from which springs a new plant. Paley, in his 'Natural Theology,' gives at length his views on the subject. Of no other plant can it be said that the roots refuse to shoot in the ground, and no other plant is known to possess this adhesive generative quality when rubbed on the branches of trees.

The seeds in germination seem to offer an exception to the general law—that the radicle or root of the embryo shoots downwards, and the plumule upwards; for it is found that the radicle of the Mistletoe invariably turns itself down upon the body to which it is attached, whatever may be the position of the surface of that body with respect to the earth. For instance, if a cannon-ball to which Mistletoe seeds are glued on all sides be suspended by a cord some distance from the earth, both the upper and under seeds, as well as those on the sides, all direct their radicle to the surface of the ball. This property insures their growing upon the branches of trees, to whatever side they may happen to adhere.

It is asserted that a branch of Mistletoe, when placed in water, has no power of absorbing this fluid, but that when the branch to which it is attached is immersed, then the water is readily absorbed and penetrates into the Mistletoe itself. The following experiment was performed by De Candolle. He immersed the branch of an apple-tree bearing Mistletoe in water previously coloured with cochineal, which, penetrating the wood and inner bark of the apple-tree, entered the Mistletoe, when its colour was even more intense than in the former.

Having no immediate connection with the earth, this curious plant, when discovered on the oak, already a sacred tree, became an object of superstitious worship to the priests of the Ancient Britons. The Druids, as they were called, held it in the greatest veneration, and the ceremony of separating the Mistletoe from the oak was one of their greatest religious rites. It was held on the sixth day of the moon, from which day they computed time. The occasion was celebrated by the sacrifice of two white bulls, which were tied to the oak-tree by their horns; then one of the Druids, clothed in white, mounted the tree, and with a knife of gold cut the Mistletoe, which was received in a "white sagum," or cloth made of wool: this done, they proceeded to their sacrifices and feastings. Our own national practice of decorating our churches and houses with Mistletoe and holly at Christmas time may, perhaps, be a remnant of the old superstition. If, however, it only be regarded as a pleasant custom, there can be no harm in it, and long may it be ere so graceful a decoration be discontinued. Sir Walter Scott, in describing Christmas in the olden times, says—

> "The hall was dress'd with holly green,
> Forth to the wood did merry men go,
> To gather in the mistletoe."

The origin of the old-fashioned tradition, that a kiss under the Mistletoe is only fair play, I am unable to find. I observe, however, as civilization advances, and manners become more polite, this practice is more honoured in the breach than the observance. In a pretty book I have had by me for many years, called 'A Wreath of Friendship,' written in part by the late Rev. Professor Henslow, when a young man, are some pretty lines on the Mistletoe. I cannot help quoting them here:—

> "Past is the time, when bending low,
> Druids revered thee, mistletoe;
> Error's broad shades are chased away
> By Revelation's brilliant ray,

PLATE IX.

MISTLETOE. *Viscum Album.* ELDER. *Sambucus Nigra.*
HONEYSUCKLE. *Lonicera Periclymenum.* YELLOW BEDSTRAW. *Galium Verum.*
GOOSE-GRASS. *Galium Assarine.* TEAZLE. *Dipsacus Fullonum.*

And superstition can no more
Bid us a humble plant adore.
Yet who in hour of Christmas mirth
Can place thee o'er the social hearth,
With ivy and with holly gay,
Or twine thee with the fragrant bay,
Nor lift with joy his heart above,
Nor hymn the notes of praise and love?
Fair plant, a mystery thy birth,
Thou dost not fix thy home on earth;
Rock'd by the winds, fed by the shower,
Thy cradle is an airy bower;
No voice of crime in thy leafy dome,
But the songs of birds to cheer thine home.
From the wilding crab this branch was riven,
From waving in the breath of heaven.
Alas! alas! they have brought it low,
To the dwellings of care, and pain, and woe."

ELDER.

SAMBUCUS NIGRA.

THE Common or Black Elder, is a small tree or large bush, belonging to the family Caprifoliaceæ. It is known by possessing a five-cleft calyx, a five-cleft rotate corolla, five stamens, and three stigmas, a roundish pulpy one-celled berry, hardly crowned by the remains of the calyx. The stem is irregularly but always oppositely branched, the young branches are clothed with a smooth grey bark, and filled with a light spongy pith; the leaflets are deep green and smooth, usually with an odd one. The flowers are in bunches of a cream-colour, with a sweetish but faint smell. The berries are black, with reddish stalks. Considerable medicinal value was at one time attributed to this plant, but it is now chiefly used in the rural districts of England for making a wine from the berries, which, when spiced and drunk hot, is regarded by some people as very agreeable. The flowers are employed in making a distilled water, which is cooling and refreshing, and is sometimes introduced into confectionery. The wood is hard and tough. The pith, on account of its solidity and great lightness, is used for making small figures and balls for electrical experiments. The undeveloped buds, when pickled, form a good substitute for capers. It is on the leaves of the elder that the caterpillar of the sphinx, or death's-head moth, delights to feed. It changes into a chrysalis about September, and in the following July may be seen as the gigantic and curious moth, with the markings of a skull on its thorax. There are two species of elder native in Britain, of which *S. Ebulus*, or Dwarf Elder, a rare plant, is the other.

HONEYSUCKLE, OR WOODBINE.

LONICERA PERICLYENUM.

THIS is a favourite flower, on account of its delicious fragrance and its lovely blossoms, intermingling with every hedge-row, and turning round the trunk of many a sturdy tree. It belongs to the family Caprifoliaceæ. The leaves are ovate or oblong, smooth above, somewhat downy or slightly hairy beneath,— the upper ones the smallest. The flowers are of a pale yellow colour, the corolla about an inch and a half long. The berries are small and red. There are two other species of honeysuckle native in Britain,— *L. Caprifolium*, the Perfoliate Honeysuckle, or Goat's-leaf, and *L. Xylosteum*, the Fly or Upright Honeysuckle.

The leaves of the perfoliate honeysuckle are quite smooth and broader than those of our example, and it flowers earlier in the year. The fly honeysuckle is rather rare; it has white scentless flowers, and is by no means so attractive as either of the others. It is often planted in shrubberies.

The true Woodbine of the poets is undoubtedly the *L. Periclymenum*; it obtains the name evidently from a corruption of *woodbind*, from its habit of twisting round the stems of trees. Milton calls it "the Twisted Eglantine," and Shakespeare says—

> "So doth the woodbine, the sweet honeysuckle,
>   Gently entwist the maple."

At the base of its long tubular flower lies the honey, and when the bee cannot reach it, other insects tap it, by making a puncture at the base of the tube, and thus regale themselves. In almost every country lane in England, from early in June to August, are we delighted with the sweet scent of one or other of these pretty climbers; and well do I remember, on a memorable occasion, becoming almost overpowered with the perfume, as bough after bough was pulled from its native Suffolk hedge, and piled up, so as to make a floral couch in a carriage in which I sat one still warm summer evening in July. Later in the year, the clusters of bright red berries, which follow the flowers, are very picturesque, and afford food for the birds; for they are not poisonous. The hawk-moth is often found hovering near the honeysuckle, attracted, perhaps, by its fragrance or feeding on the honey it contains.

YELLOW BEDSTRAW.

GALIUM VERUM.

LADIES' BEDSTRAW, or Cheese Rennet, belongs to the family Rubiaceæ. It is distinguished by having its leaves about eight in a whorl, small and linear. The stems are much branched at the base, six inches to a foot long, ending in a panicle of small golden-coloured flowers. The roots afford a rich yellow dye and impart this colour to the bones of animals who feed upon it. The whole genus possesses a property like that of rennet, of curdling milk, which gives rise to their common name. The *Galium Verum* is one of the prettiest plants, which decorates our driest sandbanks, gaily blossoming for full three quarters of the year. It is the sweetest of all the genus, and was formerly much used for strewing floors and laying in beds; whence the name of bedstraw, at a time when feather-beds and luxurious spring couches were unknown. According to John Ray, the flowering tops, when distilled, make a refreshing beverage, and the roots are useful as an astringent medicine. The French used formerly to prescribe the flowers in hysteria and epilepsy.

FULLER'S TEAZLE.

DIPSACUS FULLONUM.

THE Fuller's Teazle will be easily recognized, from our drawing, although we have one or two other British species. It belongs to the family Dipsaceæ, and is a stout biennial, four or five feet high, with numerous prickles on the stems, the leaves, and, in fact, on the whole of its surface. The heads of the flowers are of a pale lilac-colour, at first ovoid, but gradually becoming cylindrical, nearly three inches long and about one inch and a half in diameter; the scales of the involucre are hooked, or reflexed, and very hard. On this account they are used in the manufacture of cloth in a process of brushing or raising, called *teazling*. It consists in applying the ripened head or fruit of the teazle to the cloth. The teazles are attached to a cylinder, which revolves upon the cloth, and the loose particles are raised, so that they may be easily sheared or cut off, to give the cloth the fine appearance it assumes. No instrument has ever been invented to supersede the teazle. Various substitutes have been tried; pieces of wire have been fixed into a leather back, but nothing answers the purpose so well as the elastic spines of the teazle.* The plant is imported in large quantities from France and other parts of Europe, and is also extensively grown in England; but as a hot sun and dry weather are essential to the proper drying of the teazle heads, those imported from the Continent are esteemed the best. Country people are still said to cure agues in various parts of England by a singular remedy obtained from this plant, which is of course only imaginary. If the heads be opened longitudinally in the autumn, a small worm may frequently be found in the centre. Of these, three, five, or seven, always an odd number, must be taken, sealed up in a quill and worn in good faith, as an amulet or charm against ague.

* See Dr. Lankester's 'Lectures on the Uses of Animals.'

PLATE X.

CHICORY. *Cichorium Intybus.*
ELECAMPANE. *Inula Helenium.*
DAISY. *Bellis Perennis.*

SEA ASTER. *Aster Tripolium.*
CHAMOMILE. *Anthemis Nobilis.*
HAREBELL. *Campanula Rotundifolia.*

DAISY.

BELLIS PERENNIS.

THIS well-known flower is almost the first that is grasped by the hand of childhood and the last to retain its place in the floral calendar of the aged. To sit on the green grass and make daisy chains is the delight of our little ones, and the sight of the "bright-eyed, pink-tipped flower" must ever renew the associations of our youth; so it is well we should say something about it amongst the "wild flowers worth notice." The Daisy, botanically, is a typical flower of the natural order to which it belongs—Compositæ, and it is the only British species of its genus the name of which signifies perpetual beauty. Were we teaching Botany, there would be no need to describe this little flower, it is so well known all over the world; but we should with a good magnifying-glass endeavour to show that each one of the little white strap-shaped petals, as they appear to be, as well as the yellow fibres which form the centre, are in reality perfect flowers of themselves, containing all the organs that are necessary to a flower. The Daisy is not the simple flower it appears to be, but is really a great many flowers put together in one large head and held together by the little green cup, which looks like a calyx, but is not one at all. It is really a number of little bracts or leaves that grow together and form a case for the flowers inside. Under the microscope it is readily seen that the white strap is really a tube, and at one end there is a little thread ending in two horns, which is the style with two stigmas. By the aid of the glass it may also be seen that the tiny yellow threads in the centre contain the petals, with their stigmas and the little stamens growing around. A good pocket magnifying-glass adds greatly to the pleasure of a botanical ramble. The Daisy has always been a favourite with poets, both those of olden times and more modern writers. Chaucer describes himself as passing whole days leaning on his elbow and his side,

> "For nothing ellis, & I shall not lie
> But for to lokin upon the daisie
> The emprise & flowre of flowres all."

In another place he gives us the origin of the name—

> "One called eye of the daie
> The daisie, a flowre white and rede,
> And in French called La bel Margarete."

It has been said that Chaucer's frequent praises of the Daisy were intended as tributes to Margaret Countess of Pembroke, but of this there is no certain proof. The device of Margaret of Anjou, the unfortunate queen of Henry VI., was the Daisy. The French name Marguerite has reference to the resemblance of its pearly bud to the rarer pearls of the ocean. In Scotland it is called the *gowan*, and in the north of England it is recognized as the children's flower and is called "bairnwort." We all remember Wordsworth's lines on a Daisy—

> "'Tis Flora's page, in every place
> In every season, fresh and fair
> It opens with perennial grace,
> And blossoms everywhere."

Common as the Daisy is with us, it is not so in the extreme north of Europe and in America, where it is treasured as a garden flower. There is an old Celtic legend, that each new-born babe taken from earth becomes a spirit, which scatters down on the earth some new and lovely flower to cheer its bereaved parents; and there is a tale told that Malvina, who lost her infant son, was thus cheered by the virgins of Morven who came to console her:—"We have seen, oh Malvina! we have seen the infant you regret reclining on a light mist; it approached us, and shed on our fields a harvest of new flowers. Look, oh Malvina! among these flowers we distinguish one with a golden disk surrounded by silver leaves; a sweet tinge of crimson adorns its delicate rays; waved by a gentle wind we might call it a little infant playing in a green meadow, and the flower of thy bosom has given a new flower to the hills of Cromla." Since that day the daughters of Morven have consecrated the Daisy to infancy. It is called the flower of innocence; the flower of the new-born.

We all recollect the recipe of "Daisy roots and cream," prescribed by the fairy godmothers of old to stunt the growth of "ill weeds," as those were told who grew tall to their own detriment; but although there may be a sort of bitter astringent property in the daisy root, we doubt the efficacy of the dose. Gerarde, however, mentions the Daisy under the name "Bruisewort," and says it is an unfailing remedy "in all kinds of aches and pains," besides curing fevers, inflammation of the liver, and "alle the inwarde parts."

The Daisy appears almost interwoven with the materials forming the green carpet of our fields and pastures, though it is an unwelcome intruder on our velvet and closely shaven lawns, appropriated only to mossy tufts and the finest grass. Still the Daisy adapts itself to all circumstances, and can seldom be excluded from any green sward, however much care be taken to eradicate it.

CHICORY.

CICHORIUM INTYBUS.

CHICORY, or Succory, belongs to the family Compositæ. It is often seen growing wild on the borders of our corn-fields, and is sure to attract attention by its pretty blue flowers. It is from one to three feet high. The leaves near the ground are spreading, more or less hairy, with a large terminal lobe and several smaller ones, all pointed and coarsely toothed, the upper leaves smaller, less cut, and embracing the stem by pointed auricles. The flowers are in heads, in closely sessile or unstalked clusters, of a bright blue colour. When blanched, or grown without light, the leaves are often eaten in early spring salads, and are very good; they are somewhat bitter, like endive, but lose that taste by cultivation. The French call the long slender leaves "Barbe de Capuçin," Monk's Beard. The root is long, like a carrot, and is used in large quantities, when dried, as a substitute for, or an addition to, coffee. In Belgium and many parts of Germany, large districts are devoted to the cultivation of this plant for the sake of its root, which is dried in a kiln or slow oven. It is afterwards roasted like coffee, ground in a mill, and sold in the market. It is decidedly a pleasant addition to coffee; but, being much cheaper than the coffee berry, it becomes an adulteration when mixed with it and sold as pure coffee. If a teaspoonful of the powdered chicory be added to a teacupful of ground coffee, it will be found to improve the flavour, and to be in no way injurious.

THE SEA ASTER.

ASTER TRIPOLIUM.

THE Sea Aster, or Sea Starwort, is a pretty plant, found growing in salt marshes, near the coast, and belong to the family Compositæ. It is seldom above a foot high, erect or decumbent at the base; slightly branched, the leaves linear, entire, and somewhat succulent. The flower-heads are in a compact corymb; the involucral bracts few and oblong. The centre of the disk of the flower is bright yellow, the circumference blue or purple.

ELECAMPANE.

INULA HELENIUM.

ELECAMPANE is found in pastures in various parts of Europe. It is a native of Great Britain, and belongs to the order Compositæ. It has a thick, branching root, which is aromatic, bitter, and mucilaginous. The stem is three feet high, leafy, round, furrowed, solid branched, and most downy in the upper part. The leaves are large, ovate, serrated, and veiny, downy and hoary at the back; the root-leaves stalked; the rest are sessile, clasping the stem. The flower-heads are solitary, at the downy summits of the branches, two inches broad, of a bright yellow colour, with reddish streaks; the scales of the involucre are broad, recurved, leafy, finely downy on both sides. The rays are very numerous, long, and narrow, each ending in three unequal teeth. Various preparations of the boiled root have been recommended, mixed with sugar, to promote expectoration and to strengthen the stomach. Some think a spirituous extract contains most of its aromatic and tonic properties. We may generally find the plant in cottage gardens, on account of its reputed virtues. Inulin, a peculiar substance contained in the root, is a form of starch insoluble in cold water, but soluble in hot water, from which it is deposited on cooling. With iodine it gives a greenish-yellow compound which is not permanent. Inulin is distinguished from gum by its insolubility in cold water, and is otherwise chemically interesting.

CHAMOMILE.

ANTHEMIS NOBILIS.

COMMON CAMOMILE, or Chamomile, is frequently found in a wild state on many of the commons near London, where it adds a peculiar richness of colour and fragrance to the turf. It is a dwarf plant, belonging to the family Compositæ, with finely-cut leaves; the flower-heads are white in the ray, but deep yellow in the disk. All parts of the plant are intensely bitter, especially the little yellow flowers of the disk; for this reason the wild flowers are more efficacious than the cultivated sort, in which there is scarcely any disk, the white flowers of the ray having almost entirely usurped their place. An infusion or extract of these flowers is often used in medicine as a stomachic, and also as a fomentation externally. Besides the bitter principle contained in this plant, chemists have obtained from it camphor and tannin, and also a volatile oil, of a beautiful blue colour.

HAREBELL.

CAMPANULA ROTUNDIFOLIA.

No wild flower is more admired, or has had its praises sung by poets more frequently, than this pretty delicate little inhabitant of every heath and sunny bank of our country districts. Every village child loves its pretty bells, and numberless are the fancies which connect it with fairy legends and floral charms. It seems scarcely necessary to describe it botanically; but, lest it should be confounded with other species of the same genus, it may be well to say that it belongs to the family Campanulaceæ. The leaves on the tiny stem are very slender, like those of grass, but near the ground there are a number of roundish notched leaves, which mostly die away at the time of flowering. The bell-shaped corolla is of a pale blue colour, and has five broad lobes, much shorter than the entire fruit. We have nine wild species of Campanula, some of which have stout stems with large purple flowers, many of which bear the cultivation of the garden very much better than our true little Harebell, which is unhappy away from its native haunts. The Canterbury Bell, with its large handsome flowers, is one of the favourites of our gardens, and at one time abounded in the neighbourhood of Canterbury and other parts of Kent: it was gathered by pilgrims to the shrine of St. Thomas à Becket there, and treasured in evidence of the task they had completed. The little plant I have chosen as most worth notice is the true Harebell of Scotland, the same which in the 'Lady of the Lake' is mentioned as being strewn in Ellen's pathway.

> "For me she stoop'd, and looking round,
> Pluck'd a blue harebell from the ground;
> This little flower that loves the lea
> May well my simple emblem be."

It is said that the presence of the Harebell indicates a barren soil; yet how lovely are its tiny cups on their cobweb stems, gently waving to and fro with every breath of wind, so that one might almost believe in the reality of the silver music said to come from them in the days of yore, when the good fairies

> "Rang their wildering chimes to vagrant butterflies."

And even now, with all the sobering influences of botanical study upon us, we can heartily sympathize with the little one who, having filled her lap and both hands with blue bells innumerable, and *white* bells too, both growing close together, was heard to whisper in the real spirit of prayer and happiness--" Dear God, do make some pink bells too!"

BLACK WHORTLEBERRY.

VACCINIUM MYRTILLUS.

This plant, known also as Black Whortleberry, may be regarded as the representative of the British berries known as Bilberries, Cranberries, Cowberries, Windberries, &c. It belongs to the natural order or family Ericaceæ, and is a small shrub, from six inches to a foot high, with spreading green branches. The leaves fall off in the winter, and are small, ovate, with tiny teeth, and a very small stalk. The flowers are nearly round, of a pale greenish white colour, with a tinge of red, growing singly in the axils of the leaves. The berries are round, nearly black, and covered with a bluish kind of bloom, crowned by the short teeth of the calyx. This shrub is found on most mountain heaths and woods throughout England, Scotland, and Ireland, with the exception of the eastern part of England. The leaves have been much used in the adulteration of tea. The berries are frequently eaten, either in tarts or uncooked. They have a sharp astringent flavour, which is not pleasant to every one, but, like the rest of the family, they have their admirers.

The Cranberry, *V. Oxycoccus*, is well known, and is much liked in England. Great quantities of the berries are imported from Russia, Sweden, and America, into this country, packed in tubs. They are considerably

PLATE XI.

WHORTLEBERRY. *Vaccinium Myrtillus.* HEATH. *Erica Tetralix.*
HEATHER. *Calluna Vulgaris.* HOLLY. *Ilex Aquifolium.*
SPRING GENTIAN. *Gentiana Verna.* BUCKBEAN. *Menyanthes Trifoliata.*

larger and finer in appearance than those grown in our own country, but not so full of flavour.

The other species of Vaccinium are the Bog Whortleberry, *V. Uliginosum*, and the Red Whortleberry or Cowberry, *V. Vitis-idæa*.

HEATH.

ERICA TETRALIX.

THIS is the most widely distributed and best known of all our native heaths. The leaves are four in a whorl, lanceolate and linear, ciliate, downy above and on the midrib beneath. The stem is bushy at the base, with rather short, erect, flowering branches. The flowers are rose-coloured, forming little clusters or close umbels at the end of the stalks. It is commonly found in the West of Europe, and in Britain is most plentiful in the western counties. I have, however, constantly found it in Suffolk, the Isle of Wight, and other parts, often growing with the heather or *Calluna Vulgaris*, from which it is well to distinguish it. The larger and more bell-like blossoms of the Erica, and its downy appearance, are the evident marks by which we may recognize it. These heath flowers were adopted as the badges of the Highland clans; and although this heath is not especially a Scotch plant, the *Erica Tetralix* was borne by the Macdonalds, the

Erica Cinerea by the Macalisters, and the *Calluna Vulgaris* by the Macdonnells. All these plants grow together on the moors and fells in the North of England and Scotland, and give a peculiar aspect to the landscape, shedding as it were a purple hue over the distant mountains, and forming a characteristic feature of these northern districts.

There are six species of Erica in Great Britain.

HEATHER.

CALLUNA VULGARIS.

THE Heather grows, as I have said, in common with the heaths, and is often mistaken for them. Its smaller more purple blossoms, placed all along the stems in little bunches, will serve to distinguish it. Sometimes the flowers are white, but this is rare. It is especially the plant of the Highlander, and is associated so strongly with his country in all its legends and poetry, that it appears almost as exclusively the child of the mountain fastnesses as the national music of the bagpipe. To the Highlander this plant is something more than a mere badge of clanship; it furnishes him with much that is valuable in everyday life. The heather branches, freshly gathered and arranged so that the elastic tips of the shoots form a level surface, constitute a couch such as that described by Sir Walter Scott :—

> "Before the heath had lost the dew,
> This morn a couch was pull'd for you,
> On yonder mountain's purple head."

And again,—

> "The stranger's bed
> Was there of mountain heather spread."

Cabins are also thatched with it, and the walls of the cottages are often made of alternate layers of heather and a kind of mortar. As fuel it serves well, and it is said to yield a yellow dye, which I am told is at present used by the cloth-manufacturers of Yorkshire. Moreover, in England the sprigs of the heather are constantly made into brooms or besoms, which are very serviceable. As food for moor game and grouse, the heather is almost essential, and it is only where this plant will grow that these birds can be preserved. The red deer also crops the young shoots of the heather. Bees extract honey from the flowers, which though dark in colour, is very rich in flavour.

I have seen the heather, and, indeed, many species of heath, prettily used as a border for flower-beds in gardens. Sir W. Hooker suggested it, and has carried it out at Kew. Accustomed as we are in the southern districts to see the heath plants only as a low shrub, a foot or two in height, we are surprised to read of—

> "Heather black that waved so high,
> It held the copse in rivalry."

Yet so it is, and in certain wild and peaty districts it may be found quite tall enough to justify this description.

THE HOLLY.

ILEX AQUIFOLIUM.

This plant belongs to the small natural family Aquifoliaceæ, and is the only British representative of the family. It seems hardly needful to describe so well-known and favourite a tree, associated as it is with the happiest days of childhood, with Christmas-day gatherings and merry-makings, with joyous faces and warm hearts, while to some of us, perhaps, who have passed the sunshine of life, its bright green leaves and red berries may call up memories of the companions of past years, now passed away, never more to share in our joys or our sorrows. Familiar as we all are with the red berries of the Holly, we may not have seen its flowers, for they blossom when all nature is bright, and are overlooked amidst their more showy and attractive neighbours. They grow closely round the stem, and are white and wax-like, opening in May and June. The bright shining green leaves are armed with sharp prickly teeth, but the upper ones on a bush are frequently smooth. This circumstance the poet Southey impresses on the memory in his charming lines on the Holly Tree,—

> "Below a circling fence its leaves are seen,
>   Wrinkled and keen.
> No grazing cattle through their prickly round
>   Can reach to wound;
> But as they grow where nothing is to fear,
> Smooth and unarm'd the pointless leaves appear."

The tendency to produce these prickly points renders the Holly peculiarly fit for hedges, and when Dutch horticulture prevailed in England, such hedges were not unfrequent.

> "A hedge of holly, thieves that would invade,
> Repulses like a growing palisade."

The celebrated John Evelyn had such a hedge at Say's Court, four hundred feet long, nine feet high, and five feet broad, which he planted at the suggestion of Peter the Great, who resided at his house while he worked in the Deptford Dockyard. In his Diary he asks, "Is there under heaven a more glorious and refreshing sight of the kind than such an impregnable hedge, glittering with its armed and varnished leaves, the taller standards at orderly distances blushing with their natural coral?" The Holly is a very slow-growing tree, and its timber is amongst the hardest of white woods; it is much used by Turners, and especially in the manufacture of Tunbridge ware.

THE SPRING GENTIAN.
GENTIANA VERNA.

This is one of the brightest ornaments of our northern districts. It belongs to the family Gentianaceæ, and to a genus which flourishes especially in Alpine and Arctic regions. This pretty little Gentian is, however, sometimes found in warm mild districts. I have met with it in the Isle of Wight, on Shanklin Downs. Bitterness is a characteristic of the whole family, and this principle seems to have something to do with the bright blue colour of the blossoms, for the brighter the hue the more bitter the taste. Our little spring Gentian has a perennial leafy stock, densely tufted, often spreading to four or five inches in diameter, with ovate or oblong leaves. The flower-stems are simple and numerous, sometimes so short as to give the flowers the appearance of being seated on the leaves; sometimes they are an inch or two in length, and bearing one bright blue terminal flower. The corolla is tube-like, nearly an inch long, with five ovate lobes, and smaller two-cleft ones between them. The bitter principle of all the gentians is valuable as a medicinal agent.

G. Nivalis, the little Snow Gentian, grows on our loftiest mountains in Scotland and Wales, but is far better known as a native of the Alps and Pyrenees.

BUCKBEAN, OR MARSH TREFOIL.
MENYANTHES TRIFOLIATA.

THE Buckbean belongs also to the family of Gentians—Gentianaceæ. It is a beautiful aquatic herb, and is found in wet bogs and shallow ponds all over Great Britain. The stem is short, creeping, or floating, with a dense tuft of leaves, consisting each of a long stalk, sheathing at the base, and three obovate or oblong leaflets, one to one and a half inches long. The flowers are white, tinged externally with pink, in an oblong raceme on a peduncle of from six inches to a foot long, proceeding from the base of the tuft of leaves. The corolla is deeply five-lobed, and fringed on the inside with white filaments. None of our native plants exceed this in beauty. In the fresh-water aquarium it is a beautiful object, and may easily be preserved in this artificial condition for some time. In common with all its family, the Marsh Trefoil abounds in an intensely bitter quality, which has frequently been used medicinally. Withering says that the leaves have been used during a scarcity of hops as a substitute for them in brewing beer.

GREAT BINDWEED.

CONVOLVULUS SEPIUM.

THERE can scarcely be any occasion to describe this favourite and well-known plant, which wreathes its graceful festoons over our hedgerows, opening its large tender white blossoms to the bright sunshine, and gathering their folds together as a rain-cloud foretells the approach of a shower, which would shatter their delicate texture. Botanists no longer call this plant by the old name so familiar to our childhood. It is no longer the *Convolvulus*, but is known as a distinct genus, under the name *Calystegia*. The lovely white blossoms survive but for a single day; whence they are called " Belle de jour" by the French. They are, however, so rapidly succeeded by a profusion of buds ready to take their places, that the decay is not noticed, and our attention is taken off from the flower which has lived " its little day " and is now no more. A well-known author says, " How affecting an emblem of human life does this simple Convolvulus present to us. The gay, the young, whose existence has seemed but a day, are cut off, and others, equally gay and equally mortal, occupy their places ; and the remembrance of them is quickly dissipated by the attractions of their successors, who, perhaps, like them, are doomed early to submit to the common lot of humanity."

Beauty alone is not the sole merit of this plant ; the

PLATE XII.

GREAT BINDWEED. *Convolvulus Sepium.*
SKULL-CAP. *Scutellaria Galericulata.*
VIPER'S BUGLOSS. *Echium Vulgare.*

SEA BINDWEED. *Convolvulus Soldanella.*
GROUND IVY. *Nepeta Glechoma.*
FORGET-ME-NOT. *Myosotis palustris.*

root has properties similar to those of *C. Scammonia*, and has been used as its substitute under the names of Montpellier and Bourbon Scammony. It has an ancient reputation as a medicinal agent, Galen himself being said to have recommended the leaves as an external application to swellings and abscesses.

SEA BINDWEED.

CONVOLVULUS SOLDANELLA.

THIS is one of the prettiest of our sea-shore plants. It is abundant on the eastern coasts of England, on sand-hills, and flourishes well on the red clay of Suffolk and Norfolk. It belongs to the same family as the large Convolvulus, but is much smaller, trailing along the ground, and seldom rising to a height above six or eight inches. The leaves are small and kidney-shaped, with broad lobes at the base. The flower is of a delicate or bright pink colour, streaked sometimes with a darker shade. This plant shares, in common with the rest of its family, a reputation for curative properties; indeed, but few of our wild plants have not been employed in rustic pharmacy with more or less success; and it is only since the science of chemistry has proved that the active principles of these vegetable productions are the same in many different plants, and can be extracted by chemical processes, that the practice of making infusions of all sorts of herbs and weeds has been gradually abandoned for a more convenient method of administering the valuable principles to be found in nature's laboratory in smaller quantities and a less troublesome form.

VIPER'S BUGLOSS.

ECHIUM VULGARE.

THIS plant is one of the most beautiful of our wildflowers. It belongs to the family Boraginaceæ, and is known by its showy flowers, having an irregular and unequal margin, and a sort of bell-shaped figure. The red or purple spots and hairs are very remarkable. The corolla is at first of a reddish-purple colour, turning afterwards bright blue; so that there are constantly flowers of both colours to be seen at once. The whole plant is covered with stiff, spreading, almost prickly hairs. The root-leaves are stalked and spreading, but often withered away at the time of flowering. The common name of Viper's Grass originated from a resemblance the ripe seeds are supposed to have to the head of that reptile; and hence arose the idea that it might act as a remedy against the bite of the creature—an adaptation of the more recent but not less absurd fallacy that "like cures like." The showy blossoms are very attractive to bees, and not even the sharp hairs by which they are guarded are sufficient to deter these little plunderers from their depredations on the sweet store concealed in the flowers. But we must not consider these little creatures as merely selfish seekers of their own gratification; they, in common with the whole of creation, serve great purposes, and carry out the designs of the Great Architect of all, even without their own consciousness of doing so. As the insect flies from flower to flower, it transports on its delicate legs and wings some portion of the pollen which is to fertilize the next plant which it enters, and produce seed to reproduce the species. Every class of animals seem to assist in this great work of propagation in the vegetable world. Seeds are carried about by birds and deposited, as if by accident, in situations favourable for their growth; and even the giddy butterfly, as it alights on each gay flower in the sunshine, is the messenger of a new life to the rapidly-fading beauty of the garden.

FORGET-ME-NOT.

MYOSOTIS PALUSTRIS.

THIS is so entirely a flower of associations, that it is difficult to unravel anything like a botanical or prosaic description of the plant itself, from the numerous poetical fancies and legendary tales by which it is surrounded. It belongs to the Borage family—Boraginaceæ, and has small downy, ovate leaves, which are not unaptly compared to mouse-ears. Botanists, finding that the plants commonly received as Forget-me-nots differ in some minor characteristics, divide the species into three varieties. The true Forget-me-not has rather a large rotate flower, of a clear blue colour, with a yellow eye. Most abundantly does it grow beside brooks, rivers, and wayside streams, and —must we say it?—even in stagnant ditches, asking only for moisture to adorn the most deserted places with its torquoise flowers. In cultivation, it will even dispense with this requirement, and will produce blossoms of a larger size than when wild. It is an excellent plant for window gardening, and is improved by "bedding," as the gardeners call it—blossoming all the summer through, if properly trimmed. Beauty, however, is not the sole attraction of this favourite flower; it has associations connected with it in legends, in poetry, and in real life, which live long after its beautiful blossoms have perished. For many centuries it has been regarded throughout Europe as the emblem of eternal friendship or love. It is pleasant to regard so lovely a flower as expressive of a tender feeling. The well-known story is one belonging to the days of chivalry, when a knight and his lady-love were wandering on the banks of a stream where grew clusters of these gem-like flowers. In those days the wish of a love done was law to the lord: the lady, desiring to possess some of the bright blue blossoms, caused her faithful knight to rush into the stream to obtain them for her, when, overborne by the strength of the current, he was carried away, and could but cast, with dying hand, the flowers she wished for towards her, exclaiming "Forget me not." Even in our less chivalrous and more prosaic times, the language of this flower is not forgotten, and it is not long since we saw, on St. Valentine's day, when such sentiments are in fashion, and all nature is pressed into love's service, a pretty painted wreath of "Forget-me-nots" inclosed in a suitable envelope, with the words "Pretty flowers, speak for me," neatly inscribed within. One of our great botanists suggests, with a more philosophical and less poetical mind, that the real signification of the name is, after all, due to the bright blue tint and yellow eye of this charming flower, which, if once seen, is not likely to be forgotten. Nevertheless, we remain faithful to the generally-received tradition, and in justification of it, call to remembrance that as early as 1465, when a joust was held in which Lord Scales, brother to the Queen of Edward IV., took part, the fair ladies of her court presented to that favoured knight a collar of gold, enamelled with "Forget-me-nots." I am not aware that this much-prized plant has ever been used in the arts of life, yet it is a household favourite, and reminds us that there is in the human mind a deep and close association between the external beauty of nature and the strongest feelings of our hearts. Who but loves to meet, as Coleridge has it,—

> "By rivulet or wet roadside,
> That blue and bright-eyed flow'ret of the brook,
> Hope's gentle gem, the sweet Forget-me-not."

HENBANE, OR HOGSBEAN.

HYOSCYAMUS NIGER.

This belongs to the family Solanaceæ, which is chiefly characterized by its poisonous properties. Wherever there is a patch of waste ground, there may be seen the dull yellow blossoms of this dangerous plant. Its whole appearance, and the peculiar faint and disagreeable odour emitted by it, would seem almost to indicate its nature; yet the narcotic principle yielded by it is most valuable as a medicine, properly administered. It is a coarse, erect, branching annual, about one or two feet high, more or less hairy and viscid. The leaves are rather large, sessile; the upper ones clasping. The calyx is short when in flower, but points round the fruit, and is then an inch long, strongly veined, with five broad, stiff, almost prickly lobes; the stem ovate, and irregularly pinnatifid. The flowers are remarkable for their purple veins, which give them a curious appearance when in blossom, and which cause the whole plant to be peculiarly adapted for a process now not uncommon in ornamentation. If soaked for a long time in water, with some chemical agent, the soft parts of a plant decompose and disappear, leaving only the woody fibrous parts entire and bleached. These form what are known as skeleton plants, and I have seen several extremely beautiful specimens of the Henbane treated in this way, which indicates that the woody tissue is abundant in this plant. The narcotic properties of the Henbane are most strongly developed when the flowers have just fallen and the seeds are ripening. Lightfoot mentions that a few of these seeds have deprived a man of his reason and the use of his limbs; nevertheless they are frequently smoked in a tobacco-pipe as a cure for tooth-ache. The expressed juice of the plant, forming an extract, is recognized in the "Pharmacopœia," and in some cases is very valuable where other anodynes are inadmissible. A curious effect is produced on the system by these vegetable poisons, somewhat like intoxication—excitement, restlessness, and irritability are often the first symptoms of their action. A story is told of a gardener and his wife, who lived happily and in perfect contentment, until one day the good man, wishing to dry some Henbane plants, hung them up in his bedroom for that purpose. From that hour his domestic peace vanished; his wife became a perfect shrew, and he returned each curtain-lecture with interest. Happily Sir Cresswell Cresswell's court was unknown, or the speedy separation of the discontented parties would have rendered the solution of the mystery for ever impossible. Accidentally the Henbane was removed, and peace was restored. Each felt that, after all, the other was not to blame, and with returning amiability came increased happiness. It remained, however, for philosophers to trace the connection between the baneful effects of the Henbane exhalations and the irritable, quarrelsome condition of those who breathed them.

DEADLY NIGHTSHADE, OR DWALE.

ATROPA BELLADONNA.

THIS is one of our most poisonous native plants, and must be clearly described in order to be avoided. It belongs to the family Solanaceæ, and is an erect, smooth, or rather downy herb, with a perennial rootstock and branching stem. The leaves are stalked, rather large, ovate, and entire, with a smaller one usually proceeding from the same point, often so small as to look like a stipule. The flowers are solitary, on short peduncles in the forks of the stem, or the axils of the leaves. The flower is of a pale purplish-brown colour, bell-shaped, nearly an inch long. The stamens are shorter, with distinct filaments. The berries are large, and of a shining black appearance, which frequently tempts children into eating them, to their

PLATE XIII.

　　　　　 Hyoscyamus Niger.　　DEADLY NIGHTSHADE. *Atropa Belladonna.*
　　　E. *Solanum Dulcamara.*　GERMANDER SPEEDWELL. *Veronica Chama.*
　　　ON. *Antirrhinum Majus.*　GREAT MULLEIN. *Verbascum Thapsus.*

injury. The modern name, *Belladonna*, refers to the practice of the Italian *belles*, who make use of its properties to enhance their personal charms. A portion of the extract, when placed in contact with the pupil of the eye, causes it to dilate, and gives a brilliancy and lustre to these speaking orbs, which is much coveted and admired. I am told that this practice is not confined to the land of cloudless skies and southern breezes, but that in our own country the preparation is to be seen on the toilette-tables of our fashionable ladies. Happily this property is turned to good account by modern science, and in examinations of the eye it is found to be of great service in dilating the pupil, as well as previous to the operation for cataract. Numberless are the instances where death has ensued from partaking of this plant or its berries. The very powerful nature of its poisonous qualities has directed the attention of modern professors of Materia Medica towards it, and at this time it is considered to be a valuable medicinal agent. A medical friend of ours, enthusiastic in the discovery of hidden truth, not long ago nearly fell a victim to his own experiments on the action of an extract of the leaves of *Atropa Belladonna*. He had previously made known his belief that animal charcoal is the best and safest antidote to vegetable poisons. He was, however, too much under the influence of the poison to think of his own remedy, and it was only by the timely interference of a friend, who knew of the discovery, that his life was saved. It is a favourite remedy in homœopathic medicine; but as the doses given are inappreciable, it would be difficult to trace any results from their administration. The poisonous properties of this plant have long been known, as appears from its having been used by the Scotch under Macbeth to poison the Danes. Our great poet Shakespeare, with his wonderful appreciation of natural phenomena, refers, undoubtedly, to the same plant in Banquo's speech,—" Or have we eaten of the insane root that takes the reason prisoner?" Paroxysms of madness are among the curious and direful effects of this plant on the system, to which it is supposed Plutarch refers in his account of the strange and disastrous results produced on Marc Antony's soldiers "from tasting unknown herbs" when distressed for provisions.

To the same genus of plants belong the Mandrakes, *Atropa Mandragora*, the roots of which are superstitiously connected with numerous fancies, and are still sold on the continent of Europe as ingredients in love-philtres and charms. Some writers recognize them as the mandrakes of Scripture.

WOODY NIGHTSHADE, OR BITTER-SWEET.
SOLANUM DULCAMARA.

THIS belongs to the same family of plants as our last example, and is believed to have the same poisonous properties, in both fruit, leaves, and stem. This has, however, been disputed of late, and the Professor of Materia Medica at University College considers all the Solanums as perfectly innocuous. It has a shrubby stem, with climbing or strangling branches, often many feet in length, but dying far back in the winter. The leaves are stalked, ovate, or lanceolate, two or three inches long, usually broadly cordate at the base and entire, but sometimes with an additional smaller lobe or segment on each side, either quite smooth or downy on both sides, as well as the stem. The flowers are rather small, blue, with yellow anthers, in loose branches, shorter than the leaves. The berries are small, round, or ovoid, and of a bright red colour. It is to be found in hedges in shady moist situations, all over England and Ireland—more rarely in Scotland. As a medicine, this plant has been used both internally and externally; it is recommended in asthma and many other diseases.

GERMANDER SPEEDWELL.

VERONICA CHAMÆDRYS.

THIS is one of the prettiest of our wayside plants, belonging to the family Scrophulariaceæ. There are so many species of Veronica, that they are somewhat difficult to distinguish from each other. The lovely blue flower, "The Celestial Bird's-eye Blossom," as it has been called sometimes, causes it to be mistaken for the true "Forget-me-not," but those who study both will soon learn to distinguish them. The leaves are shortly stalked, ovate, cordate, crenate, and hairy. The flowers spring from the leaves on rather long stalks, and have a five-cleft calyx. The common name of Speedwell is well chosen, for what so cheering to the wayfarer as its bright blue flowers peeping out from the hedgerows to greet him as he passes by—" Stars that in earth's firmament do shine." The whole of the Veronicas have had their day in rustic medicine, and perhaps a larger list of virtues belongs to the Germander Speedwell than any of the rest. As a substitute for tea it is considered excellent by some writers. The Emperor Charles V. is said to have used it as a remedy for gout, and in cancer it is recommended by old Gerarde to be given in "Good broth of a hen," a prescription in which possibly the *vehicle* may have had more efficacy than the medicine.

In a pleasant little book by Mr. Hibberd, called

'Brambles and Bayleaves,' an anecdote connected with this charming little plant is given from the life of Rousseau, which is too interesting to remain unquoted here. "During the earliest and happiest days of Rousseau's life, he was walking with a beloved friend on a calm, serene, summer evening. The sun was setting in all its glory, spreading sheets of fire over the western sky and upon the unrippled surface of the lake, making the water still more transparent with a vivid and glowing light. The friends sat on a soft mossy bank, enjoying the calm loveliness of the scene, conversing on the varied phases of human life in the unaffected sincerity of true friendship. At their feet was a bright tuft of the lovely Germander Speedwell, covered with a profusion of brilliant blue blossoms. Rousseau's friend pointed to the little flower, the *Veronica Chamædrys*, as wearing the same expression of cheerfulness and innocence as the scene before them. Thirty years passed away! Careworn, persecuted, disappointed, acquainted with poverty and grief; known to fame, but a stranger to peace, Rousseau again visited Geneva. On such a calm and lovely evening as, thirty years before, he had conversed with the friend of his bosom, and had received a lesson from the simple beauty of a flower, he again was seated on the self-same spot.

"The scene was the same! The sun went down as before in golden majesty; the birds sang cheerfully in the soft light of eventide; the crimson clouds floated solemnly in the western sky, and the waters of the lake were calm as before. But the house wherein the first feelings of love and friendship, and the first fruits of his genius had budded, was now levelled with the ground. His dearest friend was sleeping in the grave. The generation of villagers, who had partaken of the bounty of the same beneficent hand, had passed away, and none remained to point out the green sod where that benefactor lay. He walked on pensively; the same bank, tufted with the same knot of bright-eyed speedwell, caught his eye, the memories of past years of trouble and sorrow came upon him; he heaved a sigh and turned away, weeping bitterly."

SNAPDRAGON.

ANTIRRHINUM MAJUS.

THIS is a plant belonging also to the family Scrophulariaceæ. It is frequently cultivated in gardens, but also grows wild on old walls and stony places, and on chalk cliffs in the south of England. The leaves are narrow, lanceolate, or linear entire. The flowers are large, of a purplish-red colour, or variegated with white. The corolla is above an inch long, opening like a mouth when pressed between the finger and thumb. They form perfect insect-traps; numbers of these little creatures, attracted by the sweet nectar to be found within, enter the treacherous tube, but on seeking to return, find their egress effectually prevented. Those, however, who are clever enough to gnaw a hole through the side of their prison escape uninjured. Gmelin says, that in Persia an excellent oil, equal to that of the olive, is procured from the seeds of the *A. Majus;* and Vogel observes, that the common people in many countries attribute some supernatural influence to this plant, believing it to have the power of destroying charms, and rendering maledictions of none effect. All the varieties of Snapdragon are peculiarly able to resist the effect of great droughts, and supply vegetation and beauty in situations where other flowers would perish from the power of the sun's rays.

GREAT MULLEIN.

VERBASCUM THAPSUS.

THIS plant belongs to the natural family Scrophulariaceæ, and is a stout, erect biennial, two to four feet high, clothed with soft woolly hairs, which circumstance, I believe, has given rise to its name *Verbascum*, being a corruption of *barbascum*, or bearded. The leaves are oblong, pointed, slightly toothed, narrowed at the base into two wings running a long way down the stem, the lower ones often stalked, and six or eight inches long or more. The flowers are in a dense woolly terminal spike, a foot long or more. The corolla is yellow, slightly concave; the stamens are five in number, three hairy, the other two longer and smooth. The whole plant is very showy and attractive when growing in perfection, as it sometimes does on open moors and commons. The common name Torch-blade, or King's Taper, may have arisen from its candle-like appearance when growing by itself, pointing straightly upwards, and with its flame-like crown of flowers. Some authors account for these common names rather by the fact, that the woolly covering, which is still collected for tinder, was at one time used as wicks for tapers, especially for those employed in religious services; the very trouble entailed in collecting the material seeming to recommend it for this purpose in a church where bodily sacrifices and penances are enjoined. The *Verbascum* was formerly held in high repute as a medicine in disease of the lungs; it possesses some mucilaginous sedative qualities, which caused the old herbalists to believe in it. It is one of the many herbs said to stupefy or poison fish. According to an old writer, its ashes, made into soap, will restore hair which has become grey to its original colour.

COMMON SKULL-CAP.

SCUTELLARIA GALERICULATA.

IN our summer rambles, especially on the banks of rivers or lakes and in swampy ground, we often see this little plant with its solitary bluish flowers in the axils of its bracts, and finding no resemblance to anything like a skull in it we wonder at its name. The name of the genus to which it belongs—*Scutellaria*—is supposed to have reference to the likeness of the calyx to a sort of cup with a lid to it, called *Scutella*, or perhaps to a cap or head covering.

Dr. Withering tells us that "when the blossom falls off the cup closes upon the seeds, which, when ripe, being still smaller than the cups, could not possibly escape or overcome its elastic force, and must consequently remain in useless confinement. But nature, ever fruitful of resources, finds a method to discharge them. The cup being dry divides into two distinct parts, when the seeds, already detached from the receptacle, fall to the ground."

GROUND IVY.

NEPETA GLECHOMA.

FORMERLY we used to recognize this common little plant as *Glechoma Hederaceæ* of Linnæus, but it is now put in the genus *Nepeta*, and, like the last specimen, belongs to the labiate or lipped class of plants, LABIATÆ. It is one of our commonest hedgeside plants, and abound in woods and moist shady places. It is bitter and aromatic, and when the leaves are rubbed they give out a slight scent. It used to have a reputation as a remedy for consumption, and was collected to be made into tea with that object. Until the reign of Henry VIII. it was commonly used for making beer; and, indeed, as an infusion it is by no means an unwholesome drink as a substitute for tea when the latter cannot be obtained. It is called by old English writers Ale-hoof, Gill-go-by-ground, Tun-hoof, and Cat's-foot. It is still sold in the London herb shops, but is not a remedy recognized in the Pharmacopœia. Mixed with wine it is said to take away the white specks which are sometimes seen in the eyes of horses and cows—"the pinne and wet or any griefe out of the eyes of horse or cow or any other beast"—being squirted into the same with a syringe.

BLADDER-WORT.

UTRICULARIA VULGARIS.

THE Bladder-wort is a pretty aquatic plant, abundant in our pools and water-channels, belonging to the family Lentibulaceæ. It is very remarkable for the buoy-like vesicles which are developed on its immersed leaves, and which serve to float the plant above the water. At certain seasons the whole plant is submerged, and then, if we examine these vesicles, we find them filled with water; gradually air becomes generated in the vesicles, expels the water, and the apertures are closed by a curious valve, so that the plant now becomes buoyant, and rises to the surface; the flowers expand, the seeds ripen, and then the living energy of the plant seems exhausted—air no longer fills the vesicles, but water takes its place, the plant sinks to the bottom, and the seeds are sown in their most fitting soil. The flowers are rather large, and of a yellow colour. The corolla has a short, conical, more or less curved, spur. The leaves are pinnate with numerous segments. In the eastern counties of England the Bladder-wort is not uncommon, and in many other localities it has been found, although it must be considered as rather rare.

SEA MILKWORT.

GLAUX MARITIMA.

SEA MILKWORT is common on nearly every sea-coast. It belongs to the family Primulaceæ, and is conspicuous from its rose-coloured tiny flowers, resting in the axils which its ovate fleshy opposite leaves form with its branched and procumbent stem. It is very pretty while growing, and is associated with some of our pleasantest sea-side rambles, and though scarcely attainable without incurring wet feet, it is worth the inconvenience; and those who are in health must not shrink from searching the salt marshes on the coast, for many very charming botanical treasures find their homes there.

PRIMROSE.

PRIMULA VULGARIS.

THE Primrose is a type of the natural order Primulaceæ. We select this plant because it is the real true primrose of our childhood—not the cowslip, with its deep yellow cups and nodding flowers—nor the oxlip, with its larger but paler blossoms; but the sulphur-coloured primrose with which we all associate the early days of spring, and the first ramble in the

PLATE XIV.

BLADDER-WORT. *Utricularia Vulgaris.*   MILK-WORT. *Glaux Maritima.*
PRIMROSE. *Primula Vulgaris.*   SEA COWSLIP. *Primula Officinalis.*
MONEYWORT. *Lysimachia Nummularia.*   PIMPERNEL. *Anagallis Arvensis.*

meadows or by the hedge-side. The first Primrose of the year is prized and welcomed, but when the thick tufts of its blossoms are seen, then we feel that spring is really come, and we almost fancy that no other flower ever looked so lovely or so fresh and pure. Botanically, the Primrose is an excellent example of a plant with regular monopetalous corolla, and is a good specimen for a first lesson in botany. Pretty flower as it is, all animals reject it as food excepting the pig. It seems, however, not wholly objected to by man, or woman either, for I lately saw a receipt for a primrose-pudding. A kind of wine, too, is made from the flowers, something like cowslip wine, but more delicate in flavour.

COWSLIP.

PRIMULA OFFICINALIS.

THERE seems to be no reason for describing the Cowslip, for I suppose every one knows it as an old friend of childhood, as well as its relative the primrose, or its frequent companion the daisy. It belongs, as may be almost inferred, to the same natural order as the primrose—Primulaceæ, and there is evidently a tendency in the one species to run into the other. We have seen specimens of primroses becoming small, and growing two or three on a stalk, on a plant bearing single-stalked primroses, and cowslip flowers on single short stalks, amidst the tiny clusters of cups usually found on a Cowslip stalk. In some country places the Cowslip is called the Paigle. Its flowers contain a quantity of honey, and possess some very slight narcotic properties which has induced the idea that an infusion of them is good as a medicine. Cowslip wine is a favourite country febrifuge, and is given to children in all sorts of feverish attacks, such as measles and the like. The gathering of Cowslip flowers forms quite an occupation in Worcestershire, where they are sold by measure to the British winemakers of that part of the country. They are fermented with sugar and water, and when well prepared are really not unpalatable. The sedative qualities of the plant are sufficient to have procured for it the reputation of an anodyne, and we find Pope writing—

> "For want of rest
> Lettuce and cowslip; probatum est."

Montgomery also alludes to the process of wine-making from the flowers—

> "Whose simple sweets with curious skill
> The frugal cottage dames distil,
> Nor envy France the vine,
> While many a festal cup they fill
> With Britain's homely wine."

The root of the Cowslip is also astringent and diuretic, and was at one time used medicinally. It has a scent resembling anise, and was at one time esteemed as a perfume in some parts of Europe. The leaves are perfectly wholesome, and may be eaten as a potherb or a salad.

MONEYWORT, OR CREEPING LOOSE-STRIFE.
LYSIMACHIA NUMMULARIA.

THIS is a pretty little plant, to be seen in all hedges, or on banks, during the summer and autumn, throughout England. It belongs to the natural family Primulaceæ. The stems are prostrate, trailing to the length of one or two feet, often rooting at the nodes. The leaves are round, on very short stalks, looking almost like pieces of money; the flowers yellow, large, and handsome, on short stalks—the segments of the calyx are pear-shaped. With a microscope little pedicillate glands may be seen covering the blossoms and stamens.

PIMPERNEL, OR POOR MAN'S WEATHER-GLASS.
ANAGALLIS ARVENSIS.

> "Whose brilliant flower,
> Closes against the approaching shower,
> Warning the swain to sheltering bower,
> From humid air secure."

THIS well-known and very attractive little plant belongs to the family Primulaceæ, and is a neat, much-branched, procumbent annual, six inches to near a foot long, with opposite, broadly ovate, sessile, and entire leaves. The calyx divisions are pointed. The corolla is rotate, and usually of a bright red colour; sometimes it is white or pale pink, or blue. The blue variety is as common in central and southern Europe as the red is with us, but in England it is very rare. I have, however, found it in Suffolk, in a lane near Felixstowe, where the red Pimpernel grows most luxuriantly. The extreme sensitiveness of this pretty little plant to a change of atmosphere causes it to shut up its petals at the approach of rain. In fine weather it remains open from about eight in the morning till four in the afternoon. It is a common weed in the valley of the Nile, and its botanical name, which is derived from the Greek, signifies a "reviver of the spirits," in allusion to the medical and magical properties for which it was at one time highly valued. At present its only use seems to be as a pot-herb, and it is also sometimes—more especially on the Continent—eaten as a salad.

PLANTAIN, OR WAY-BREAD.

PLANTAGO MAJOR.

THOUGH not an attractive-looking plant as we generally see it by the wayside, it is so closely associated with almost every walk along a country lane, or even

PLATE XV.

GREAT PLANTAIN. *Plantago Major.*   PURPLE SPURGE. *Euphorbia Peplis.*
WATER STAR-WORT. *Callitriche Verna.* COMMON NETTLE. *Urtica Dioica.*
BLACK BRYONY. *Tamus Communis.*   WATER SOLDIER. *Stratiotes Aloides.*

high-road, that it can scarcely escape notice. The leaves are erect or spreading, broadly ovate, entire or toothed, on longish channelled stalks. The peduncles are usually longer than the leaves, bearing a long slender spike of sessile flowers. The sepals are green in the centre, the stamens longer than the corolla; the whole flower is small, white, with pinkish anthers. In general the Plantains are regarded merely as troublesome weeds. Their leaves are eaten by some animals, but contain very little nutriment. The common name of *P. Major* is undoubtedly Way-bred, not Way-bread, as it is usually spelt, from its frequency by the way-side, seeming as if bred on the road. This plant has a peculiar tendency to follow the migrations of man, as if domestically or sympathetically attached to the human race, and has followed our colonists to every part of the world; so that it has been named by the natives in some of our settlements "The Englishman's foot," for with a strange degree of certainty it is found wherever our countrymen have trod. It is a favourite food with birds, and nothing delights them more when kept in confinement than a supply of the long stalks of Plantain to peck at. In the summer, when a supply of other green food can be found for our favourites, the Plantain is not so much sought for; but it should be gathered and laid by in store for the winter, when it will be a treat to the little inhabitants of our aviaries. Bruised Plantain leaves are esteemed an excellent remedy for cuts and bruises, and also as an application to the bites of stinging insects. In the Highlands of Scotland an ointment is made from them, which is said to be very efficacious. There are five British species of Plantain, some of which have medicinal reputation from their mucilaginous properties. *P. Coronopus* has been eaten as a salad, but is too bitter to be pleasant.

PURPLE SPURGE.

EUPHORBIA PEPLIS.

THIS is a handsome plant belonging to the family Euphorbiaceæ. It is found only on the sea-coasts, and is becoming rare in Great Britain. It loses all its leaves before flowering, when the short main stem divides close to the base, so that the whole plant appears to consist of the forked procumbent branches lying on the sand in patches from six inches to a foot in diameter. The whole plant has a reddish or purplish hue, and that peculiar glaucous appearance so general in sea-shore plants. The leaves are opposite, half oblong, heart-shaped, and very thick, with small stipules at their base. The flower heads are very small. The genus Euphorbia is a very extensive one; there are fourteen or fifteen British species, nearly all of which have an acrid poisonous secretion.

A notion prevails that milk is an antidote to this poison, but without reason, as we read in Withering's botany of a strong youth who was poisoned by drinking milk in which the plant had been boiled. As a cure for warts we can believe in the virtues of the Spurge; its astringent or acrid qualities may have some powerful effect as an external application; but old Gerarde's advice is certainly worthy quoting, where he says: "These herbes by mine advise would not be received into the body, considering that there be so many good and wholesome potions to be made with other herbes that may be droken without perill." The ancient Britons used the Euphorbia to poison fish, which practice is continued by the Abyssinians. It is said that the fish thus killed are good for food, but this is doubtful, as there are instances of people being poisoned merely from drinking the milk of a goat which had fed on the Euphorbia.

WATER STAR-WORT.

CALLITRICHE VERNA.

THIS is the representative of the only genus of Water Star-worts—Callitrichaceæ—in Great Britain. This pretty plant is very suitable for the aquavivarium, and is found in stagnant and slowly-running water all over the country. It is easily known by its upper leaves floating on the water, and two or three pairs of them forming a little green star, hence its name. This plant forms a beautiful object under the microscope, for its leaves and stem are covered with very minute rosette-shaped bodies, which seem to supply the place of hairs in other plants. There are other species of Water Star-wort in England, but they are much more rare.

COMMON NETTLE.

URTICA DIOICA.

THE very name of the genus of plants to which the Nettle belongs indicates its peculiar property. It comes from the Latin word *uro*, I burn, and but few there are on whom it has not at some time or other impressed itself and its properties on their memory. The appearance of the leaves of the Nettle are well known, beset with numerous tiny hairs, each furnished with a little receptacle at their base, which exudes an acrid fluid when touched, causing pain and inflammation to the skin. Bad as are the stings of our ordinary common Nettle, they are nothing as compared with those of the great Roman Nettle—*Urtica Pilulifera*—which is found chiefly near the sea. Camden relates, that when Julius Cæsar landed on Romney marshes the soldiers brought some of the Nettle seed with them and sowed it for their use—"to rub and chafe their limbs when, through extreme cold, they should be stiff and benumbed; being told before they came from home that the climate of Britain was so cold that it was not to be endured without some friction to warm their blood." Certainly rather than use Nettles in this way, one would prefer to live in the parish of Dreepdaily, where they "force Nettles for early spring Kail."

We are told that Nettles, dressed like spinach, are excellent, and they may be earthed up and blanched in the same way as sea-kale, when they form a very palatable vegetable. Cattle do not eat Nettles when growing or fresh gathered, but when dried in hay do not refuse them.

The juice of Nettles yields a beautiful permanent green dye which is used in Russia for woollen stuffs. The fibres of the plant are strong, and can be woven into textile fabrics. Campbell, the Scotchman who complains of the neglect with which Nettles are treated in England, says, "In Scotland I have eaten Nettles, slept in Nettle-sheets, and dined off a Nettle table-cloth." The fibre is more difficult to prepare for weaving than that of flax, otherwise it might have found more favour as a fabric in Britain.

Goldsmith mentions a curious application of Nettle properties in rearing young chickens. He tells us to catch a young capon, strip his breast of feathers, and then rub it with Nettle leaves; put a brood of chickens under him, which presently run under his breast, and, rubbing his bare skin gently with their heads, allay the stinging caused by the Nettles. This process, if repeated for a few nights, causes the capon to take an affection to the chickens that have thus given him relief, and he continues to afford them the protection they seek, and will from that time bring them up like a hen with the tenderest care.

Nettle tea is a country remedy, well known, and thought to be very efficacious in the early spring. It is, however, possible that the Nettles themselves boiled and eaten might be equally beneficial and more agreeable, for it is certain in most cases that a large proportion of vegetable diet is likely to contribute to good health.

BLACK BRYONY.

TAMUS COMMUNIS.

This is an elegant climbing plant, which through the whole summer may be seen festooning our hedges and bushes. Its bright shining heart-shaped leaves clothe the trunks of many of our sturdy old trees with a verdure unequalled by any other plant. The lightness of its twining stems prevents it from injuring the branches within its grasp, for they have not the firmness or strength of the ivy, which is sometimes too close in its embrace.* The flowers are unattractive and small, but the berries of the Bryony, hanging like clusters of wild green grapes during the summer, and changing into brilliant scarlet balls in the autumn, are objects of great beauty. They are very poisonous, and must not mislead by their charming appearance. The early shoots of the plant, however, have frequently been boiled and eaten, it is said, with great relish and with no bad results. The roots have a black colour externally, hence the name of the plant. The interior is white and full of starch, which is, however, bitter and unwholesome. The acrid pulp of these roots has been used as a stimulating plaster.

WATER SOLDIER.

STRATIOTES ALOIDES.

THIS plant, so named from its sword-shaped spring leaves and fancifully military appearance, is a very ornamental aquatic plant. It belongs to the family Hydrocharidaceæ, and is found very abundantly in lakes and watery ditches in the east of England. In Norfolk and Suffolk it is very plentiful, and is an interesting

* The family Dioscoreaceæ, to which the Tamus belongs, includes the yams; the tubers of which are well known as an article of food in South Africa and Mexico, and have lately been extensively sent to England, but, as yet, are not very popular, so great is the prejudice against any innovation on our old habits in diet.

plant to observe. It remains submerged during the greater part of the year, but raises itself to the surface on special stalks during the season for fertilizing the seeds. It forms a favourite hiding-place for multitudes of aquatic insects, as may be seen if a plant be quickly raised out of the water. The whole plant seems to resemble an aloe more than anything else, and is equally rigid and sharp in its leaves.

EARLY ORCHIS.

ORCHIS MASCULA.

WE now come to a most attractive and beautiful group of wild flowers, difficult to describe, and very puzzling to the young botanist, but easily recognized by any one who has seen and gathered them, even without knowing their scientific distinctions. The Early Orchis blossoms in the months of May and June, and may be found in any meadow or moist wood throughout Great Britain. The stem is a foot or a foot and a half high, bearing numerous showy flowers, in a loose spike, from three to six inches long, varying in colour from a pinkish purple to flesh-colour, or even white. The leaves are broad and often spotted with purple. The bracts are coloured nearly as long as the ovary, with a single rib. The upper sepal and the petals converge over the ovary, but the lateral sepals are spreading, or turned

PLATE XVI.

EARLY ORCHIS. *Orchis Mascula.*
BEE ORCHIS. *Ophrys Apifera.*
YELLOW IRIS. *Iris Pseudacorus.*

MAN ORCHIS. *Orchis Militaris.*
FLY ORCHIS *Ophrys Muscifera.*
DAFFODIL. *Narcissus Pseudonarcissus.*

back. The lip is scarcely longer than the sepals, often slightly downy in the centre, turned back on each side with three short lobes, the middle one the largest. The tubers of all the Orchis plants contain a good deal of farinaceous nutritious matter, consisting, according to modern chemists, of a principle called Bassorin. This substance is commonly known as *saloop*, or *salep*, a word derived from the Persian name of the Orchis, which, according to Forskhale, is *sahleb*. When boiled in water, it used to be sold at the corners of the streets in London, and was a favourite drink with coal-heavers, porters, and other hard-working men. It is still highly esteemed in the East; and during the Great Exhibition of 1851 was exhibited and sold as a beverage. It is said to contain more nutritious matter according to its bulk than any other vegetable substance, and that an ounce a day will sustain a man; hence it is a favourite food, from its portability, with pedestrian travellers in wild deserts and uninhabited countries.

MAN, OR MILITARY ORCHIS.

ORCHIS MILITARIS.

THIS is a handsome species of Orchis, from one to two feet high, with entire tubers. It is difficult to say what fancy has given rise to the name; the red colour of the flowers or the shape of the root may have suggested a soldier-like resemblance. The leaves in the lower part of the stem vary from broadly oval to oblong; they are usually three to five inches long. The flowers are numerous, in a dense oblong spike, with short bracts. The sepals are red or purple, and converge over the petals and column in the shape of a helmet. The lip is more or less spotted with rough, red points, and four-lobed, or rather *three*-lobed, with two entire lobes, and a third one divided in the middle into two, with a small tooth in the cleft or notch. It is found on chalky hills, on the borders of woods, and in hilly pastures. Near London it should be looked for about Dorking, Rochester, and Northfleet. There are very many other British Orchises; all of them are pretty and attractive, and one, *A. Conopsea*, has a fragrant, agreeable scent.

BEE ORCHIS.

OPHRYS APIFERA.

THIS plant belongs to the family Orchidaceæ, and to a section of that family most curiously eccentric in the forms of its flowers, very closely resembling the Orchises with the habits, tubers, and foliage of that group of plants; but the flowers of Ophrys have no spur, and the lip is usually very curved, resembling,

more or less, the body of an insect. They are often
called Orchis, though not properly belonging to that
genus. The Bee Orchis blossoms in July, in dry
pastures, in chalky and limestone districts. In the
eastern counties of England it is not uncommon. It
has a brown, velvety lip, variegated with yellow, which
resembles the body of a bee; the purplish petals look
like the expanded wings of an insect which had just
settled on the stem of the flower. Langhorne's pretty
lines have been often quoted, but are too descriptive
to be omitted here :—

> "See on the flow'ret's velvet breast
>   How close the busy vagrant lies,
> His thin-wrought plume, his downy breast,
>   The ambrosial gold that swells his thighs.
> Perhaps his fragrant load may bind
>   His limbs—we'll set the captive free;
> I sought a living bee to find,
>   And found the picture of a bee."

FLY ORCHIS.

OPHRYS MUSCIFERA.

This is a much more delicate, slender plant than the
Bee Orchis, with narrow leaves and a slender spike of
three or four flowers. The sepals are whitish-green;
the lips brownish-purple, oblong, convex, and with
pale blue or white marks in the centre; the two lateral
lobes turned down; the central one large, with a deep

notch. The blue spot upon the base of the middle segment of the lip contributes much to the resemblance of the flower to a fly, which, indeed, is singularly close. We have also in this genus of plants the Spider Ophrys; and there is also the Butterfly Orchis, and the Lizard Orchis; these latter names are not, however, so well applied as those of the bee and fly.

YELLOW FLAG—WATER FLAG.

IRIS PSEUDACORUS.

THE Flag plant is found in wet meadows and marshes and along water-courses throughout Europe. It belongs to the family Iridaceæ. The stem is about two feet high. The lower leaves are often much longer, stiff and erect, and of a pale green colour; the upper leaves are shorter. The flowers proceed from a sheathing bract, are large, erect, and of a bright yellow colour, two or three together. The stigmas are petal-like, rather longer than the inner segments, two-cleft at the top, with a short scale-like appendage inside at the base of the lobes. The capsule is green, from two to three inches long, with numerous pale brown seeds. The medicinal uses of this plant are various. The juice of the fresh root is very acrid, and acts powerfully. Withering mentions a case where it was given to some swine bitten by a mad dog, and they escaped the disease; while some others, bitten by the same dog, died with all the symptoms of hydrophobia: but I need not say that unless some evidence existed of this plant possessing active properties, Withering's cases do not prove any connection between the medicine and the cure It is on such reasoning as this that many medical fallacies are based. The roasted seeds are said to be a good substitute for coffee, when carefully prepared. Few plants can exceed the Iris in elegance of form; in our gardens it is a great ornament, and by the sides of streams and lakes it should always be encouraged

> "Amid its waving swords,
> In flaming gold the Iris towers."

The Iris is undoubtedly the original of the *fleur de lys* in the arms of France, and in many pieces of sculpture in which this device is introduced, it is not difficult to recognize it. The plant was considered in ancient times as peculiarly sacred to the Virgin Mary, as shown in the old legend of the knight who, more devout than learned, could never retain in his memory more than two words of a prayer to the Lady Mother. These were *Ave Maria*, and with these he constantly addressed his prayer to Heaven. Night and day his prayer continued, until the good old knight died and was laid in the chapel yard of the convent, when, as a proof of the acceptance of his brief though earnest prayer, a plant of *fleur de lys* sprang up on his grave displaying on every flower in golden letters the words *Ave Maria*. The sight induced the monks, who had despised him during his lifetime on account of his ignorance, to open his grave; and there they found the root of the plant resting on the lips of the good old soldier who lay mouldering there.

In Britain we find but two really native species of Iris, *I. Pseudacorus* and *I. Fœtidissima*, the smell of the crushed leaves of which is thought to resemble roast beef; tastes differ, however, for Linnæus, when he gave the specific name, must have regarded it as anything but savoury in smell. The juice is sometimes used to excite sneezing in cases of headache, but it is a very unsafe practice.

DAFFODIL—DAFFY-DOWN-DILLY.

NARCISSUS PSEUDONARCISSUS.

THIS is a well-known pretty plant, belonging to the family Amaryllidaceæ. The name Narcissus seems to be wrongly applied to this species, as it belongs, no doubt, to the *Narcissus Pocticus* of the Greeks, which has a flower with a very powerful scent, a quality from which the daffodil is free. The Narcissus was consecrated to the Furies, who stupefied their victims, hence Sophocles calls these flowers "garlands of the infernal gods." The fable of the youth Narcissus, after whom the plant is named, is well known to everybody; how he fell in love with his own image reflected in the water, and pined away until he was changed into the pale flower which rightfully bears his name. Our present specimen, the Daffodil, bears simply the old English name *affo dyle*, which signified "that which cometh early," and it was long before the word was corrupted into *daffodil*. It is one of our earliest spring flowers; it is rare in Scotland and Ireland, but in the south-west of England its yellow or pale lemon-coloured blossoms may be seen covering acres of land. In Cornwall they are still called Lent lilies. The root, and, to some extent, the whole plant, is poisonous, yet a useful spirit is distilled from it, which has been used as an embrocation, and also given as a medicine. Most welcome are these pretty spring flowers to us all, and in cottage gardens they add beauty and grace without expense or trouble, for they grow under almost any conditions.

> "When the vales are decked with daffodils,
> I hail the new reviving year,
> And soothing hope my bosom fills."

WILD HYACINTH.

HYACINTHUS NONSCRIPTUS.

This well-known pretty plant is known to every child who has rambled in the fields and woods in search of wild flowers. It is sometimes called the Harebell, or Bluebell, but is quite distinct from the *Campanula Rotundifolia*, the true Bluebell of Scotland. It belongs to the family Liliaceæ, and by some botanists is not called Hyacinth at all, but is placed with the squills, and is called *Scilla Nutans*. It is the child of the spring and the denizen of the woods, whilst the *Campanula* is the pride of harvest time, and flourishes in exposed situations. The wild Hyacinth has a white bulb, full of clammy juice. The leaves are linear, shorter than the flower-stem. The stem is about a foot high, angular, with a terminal one-sided raceme of drooping blue flowers, each with a small narrow bract at the base of the pedicel. We all know the beautiful sweet-scented Hyacinth of the gardens, but nothing can be more charming than the masses of these wild blue Hyacinths sometimes seen in sheltered places under the spreading branches of trees, forming almost a living carpeting to some shady nook. In Kew Park, acres of the green grass is changed from green to blue by the presence of these lovely blue flowers. The *Hyacinthus Nonscriptus* is not the true Hyacinth of ancient Greek story; that is supposed to have been a

PLATE XVII.

WILD HYACINTH. *Hyacinthus Nonscriptus.* GRAPE HYACINTH. *Muscari Racemosum.*
SPRING SQUILL. *Scilla Verna.* TURK'S-CAP LILY. *Lilium Martagon.*
SNAKESHEAD LILY. *Fritillaria Meleagris.* MEADOW SAFFRON. *Colchicum Autumna*

species of Lily, which sprung from the blood of the beautiful boy Hyacinthus, whom Apollo unfortunately killed; so that though we cannot claim for our favourite a place in classic lore, we think that its own unassuming beauty, delicate scent, and the early associations it must recall to all hearts, will justify its introduction here. The juice contained in the root of the Hyacinth is sometimes used as starch or gum. At one time, when stiff ruffs were worn, it was much in request. It also served the purpose of the book-binder, to fasten the covers of books securely.

GRAPE HYACINTH.

MUSCARI RACEMOSUM.

THE Grape Hyacinth belongs to the order Liliaceæ, but may be easily distinguished from our common Hyacinth, although belonging to the same family, and flowering about the same time. The leaves are narrow, lanceolate, rather thick, not stiff, from six inches to a foot long, or, when very luxuriant, a foot and a half long. The stem is usually shorter, with a close terminal raceme, or head of small, dark-blue flowers, looking almost like little berries; a few of the uppermost are of a paler blue, erect, much narrower, and without stamens or pistil. At one time this plant was very much cultivated in gardens. It abounds in sandy soils, and is plentiful in the eastern counties of England.

SPRING SQUILL.
SCILLA VERNA.

This plant belongs also to the family Liliaceæ, and is a pretty plant, found chiefly in the north and west coasts of England, near the sea. In Wales it has, however, been frequently met with, and on the east coast of Ireland, but rarely in Scotland. It is a delicate little plant, with a small bulb, and narrow, linear leaves, two to four inches long. The flower-stem is seldom above six inches long, with several small, erect, blue flowers, in a short terminal raceme, almost forming a corymb. The blossoms are bell-shaped, but not pendant, and of a bluish-violet colour. The foreign species of Squills have long been celebrated for their medicinal qualities, but I am not aware that any properties of a like kind have been attributed to their British relatives.

SNAKESHEAD LILY, OR COMMON FRITILLARY.
FRITILLARIA MELEAGRIS.

This pretty plant belongs to the Lily tribe—Liliaceæ; indeed, this is so beautiful a family of plants, that it is difficult not to show a partiality to it when choosing wild flowers "worth notice." The Fritillary is not a common plant; it is found chiefly in the southern and eastern counties of England, and cannot be said to be wild at all in Scotland. The unexpanded blossom, somewhat fancifully, is said to resemble a snake's head; hence its common name. It has a stem about a foot high, with its leaves alternate and linear lanceolate; the single drooping flower, of a dull red colour, marked curiously with pink and dark purple; hence the name *Fritillaria*, from *Fritillus*, a dice-box—the frequent companion of a cheque or checkered board. It blossoms in April, in meadows and pastures throughout England, and is the only British species of the genus. In the season the meadows of Christ Church, Oxford, are covered with these beautiful flowers. Many handsome foreign species are cultivated in our gardens. The handsome Crown Imperial (*Fritillaria Imperialis*) is a native of Persia, and belongs to the Tulip group of the liliaceous tribe of plants.

TURK'S-CAP LILY.

LILIUM MARTAGON.

THIS belongs to the Tulip group of the Lily family of plants. It is not a common plant in its wild state, though in gardens it is cultivated to great perfection and beauty. It is to be met with, however, on chalk hills and in woody places in the southern parts of England. The scent of the Lily is so powerful as to be very annoying to some people, though in this species, and in their wild state, it is not so perceptible. The flower may readily be recognized, from its common name. The petals are reflexed, and turn over, forming a sort of turban, while the stamens appear like a tuft of feathers at the top.

MEADOW SAFFRON.

COLCHICUM AUTUMNALE.

In the autumn of the year, when all nature seems losing her brilliancy, and the "sear and yellow leaf" proclaims the approach of winter, this pretty flower forms a gay carpet in the fields and meadows. It may easily be mistaken for a crocus, which, however, belongs to a different family, and blossoms in the spring of the year.

> "The Crocus blows before the shrine,
> At vernal dawn of St. Valentine."

The Colchicum belongs to the family Melanthaceæ, while the crocus is placed with the Iridaceæ. The flowers of the Colchicum are large, of a pale purple colour, and spring up without leaves, forcing their way through the soil, and expanding just above the ground, leaving the tubular part with the ovary and filaments enveloped in membranous sheathing spathes below the soil. Each stalk produces six or eight of these flowers. The stamens are six, the ovaries three, each with a long thread-shaped style, and not adhering in any manner to the flower. These are succeeded by the fruit in the form of three little follicles, which slightly adhere together by their inner edge, and in the spring are elevated above the soil by their lengthened footstalk. At this time too the foliage makes its appearance in the form of an erect tuft of oblong shining sheathing leaves. Each follicle contains several oblong seeds. So like is the whole plant to the autumn crocus, that inexperienced observers may readily mistake one for the other. They may be distinguished, however, by remembering that the crocus has only three stamens, one style, and an inferior ovary; while the Colchicum has six stamens, three styles, and a superior ovary. The crocus, too, is perfectly free from those poisonous qualities which distinguish the Colchicum, and render it so useful a plant in medicine. Many species of Colchicum are cultivated for the sake of their flowers, and are badly distinguished by botanists from our specimen, which alone is of any worth in materia medica. So virulent are the poisonous properties of the *C. Autumnale*, that the fingers are sometimes benumbed in preparing it, and cattle which have been driven to eat it through hunger have frequently died. It is very important for those who are employed in collecting the plant for medicinal use, to know that the active principle it contains appears to become concentrated in different parts of the plant at different seasons of the year. In June and July the root is in perfection; in September the flowers, and the seeds in the following spring. No vegetable poison has been more advantageously applied in medicine than this. Sir Everard Home recommended a tincture of it as efficacious in curing the gout, and it is now even more generally prescribed in rheumatism and gout than in his time. The Hermodactyl of the Greeks is believed to have been a species of Colchicum; it was celebrated as a remedy for gout in ancient times, and its celebrity has been again revived as an ingredient in the French remedy—"*Eau Médicinale.*"

FLOWERING RUSH.

BUTOMUS UMBELLATUS.

THIS is a peculiarly elegant plant, belonging to the family Alismaceæ. It is a rush-like plant, with three-cornered, sword-shaped leaves, and umbels of handsome rose-coloured flowers containing nine stamens, a peculiarity by which it is immediately recognized among other wild flowers. The roots are regarded in Russia as a specific in hydrophobia, but experiments made with them in this country have not confirmed the accounts given of their properties by Russian physicians, and they do not seem to offer any remedy for this terrible and incurable disease. Well may the name of this beautiful plant signify the " Pride of the Water:" it is one of the most ornamental natural adornments of our lakes and rivers, and in marshy districts, where all looks barren and desolate, there may be seen the bright-coloured flowers of the Flowering Rush, by their beauty making " the wilderness to rejoice and blossom as the rose."

Withering quotes a couplet, which is expressive and true :—

> " Her rosy umbels rears the Flowering Rush,
> While with reflected charms the waters blush."

COMMON ARROW-HEAD.

SAGITTARIA SAGITTIFOLIA.

THIS plant belongs to the family Alismaceæ, but differs from some other genera of that family in having unisexual flowers. The leaves, which are arrow-shaped, rise out of the water on very long stalks, the blades six or eight inches long. The flower-stem is leafless, erect and longer than the leaves—bearing on its upper part several distinct whorls of rather large white flowers with a purplish tinge at the base of the petals; but so readily do they fall off, that it is difficult to preserve them. The upper flowers are those which contain the stamens, the lower ones on shorter stalks contain the pistils. There is but one locality in Scotland recorded where this plant is growing wild; that is somewhere near Paisley. In England and Ireland it is not uncommon, and may be seen in luxuriance on the banks of the Thames, above Putney, during the summer and autumn. The roots of this plant, as well as those of other species, contain an amylaceous matter, which is said to form a nutritious food, and is eaten for that purpose by the Chinese and Kalmuk Tartars.

CUCKOO PINT,—LORDS AND LADIES.

ARUM MACULATUM.

CAN we wonder at the delight of country children with this curious plant, which seems almost to be one of those things we constantly see in nature, designed to illustrate the grotesque as well as the beautiful. Its large handsome spathe, rising up amidst the elegantly-shaped spotted leaves, forms a fitting shelter for the bright-coloured spadil or flower-stalk, the lord or lady, whichever it may be, within its protecting hood. The plant belongs to the family Araceæ, and is the only representative of its family found wild in this country. It would puzzle the beginner in botany to make out the parts of the flower corresponding to

PLATE XVIII.

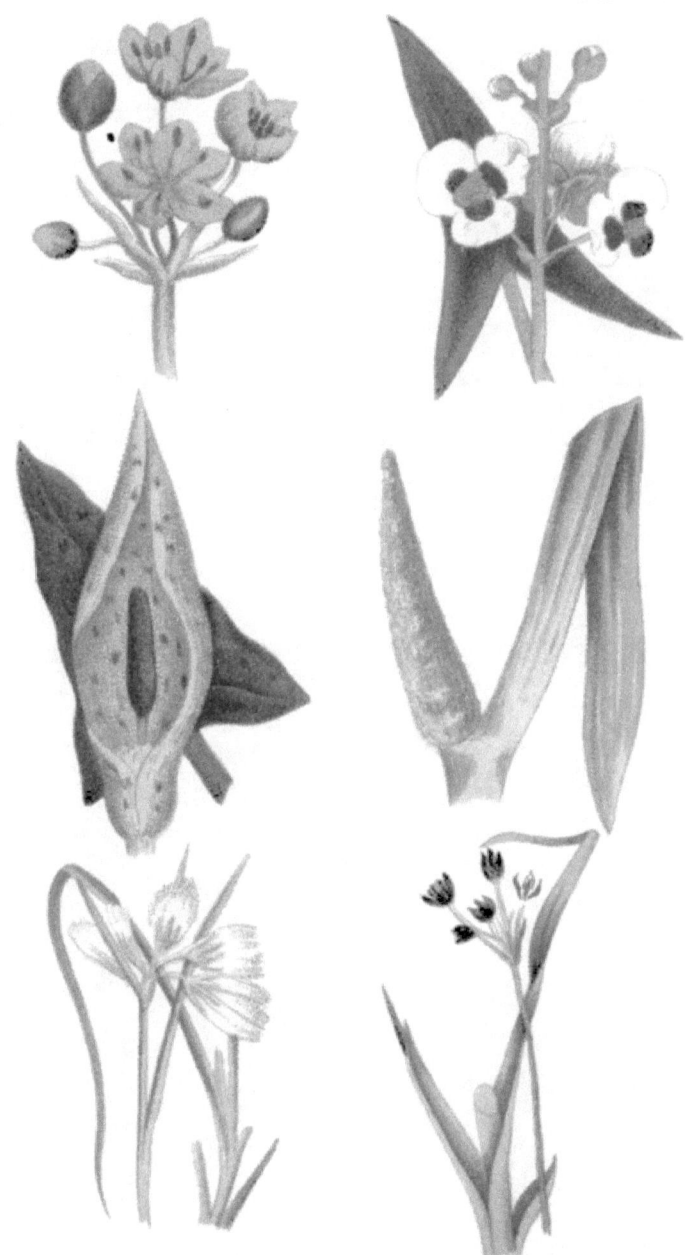

FLOWERING RUSH. *Butomus umbellatus.*
CUCKOO PINT. *Arum Maculatum.*
COTTON GRASS. *Eriophorum Angustifolium.*
ARROW-HEAD. *Sagittaria Sagittif*
SWEET FLAG. *Acorus Calamus.*
BULRUSH. *Scirpus lacustris.*

those of a Primrose, but after a little study they will be easily understood. The attraction of this curious plant does not cease after the early spring, when the green leaves have faded away, and the lords and ladies and their habitation are no more seen; the little bunch of seedlike bodies about half-way down the coloured spadil, which are in fact the pistils and seed-vessels, in the autumn of the year assume a brilliant red colour, looking like a bunch of coral, as amid the withering grass of some hedge-side they attract the notice of the passer-by; beware, however, of being tempted to taste them. The whole plant is acrid, pungent, and poisonous. The tubers contain a sort of farinaceous substance, which, when freed from its acrid qualities, constitutes a nutritious article of diet. Large quantities are collected in Portland Island and on the dry and sunburnt districts on the banks of the Bristol Channel, and sold under the name of Portland sago. It is largely used to adulterate arrowroot. On the Continent its economical uses appear to be generally known and appreciated. Dr. Withering quotes Wedelius for the supposition that it was on this plant, under the name of Chara, on which the soldiers of Cæsar's army subsisted when encamped at Dyrrachium. A curious belief is recorded by Gerarde as coming from Aristotle, that when bears were half-starved with hybernating, and have lain in their dens forty days without any nourishment but such as they get by "sucking their paws," they were completely and suddenly restored by eating this plant. Medicinally the Arum had at one time a great reputation in common with all other plants containing acrid or poisonous principles. In rheumatism, gout, and even consumption, its virtues were vaunted, but are now happily discarded. The Arum is one of those plants which exhibits the curious and interesting fact of the vegetable evolution of heat, so evident, that for some hours after the opening of the spathe it may be felt with the hand or tested with the thermometer.

COMMON COTTON GRASS.

ERIOPHORUM ANGUSTIFOLIUM.

THE appearance of this pretty plant, which belongs to the natural order *Cyperaceæ*, is well known to all who have made excursions in the early part of the year in moorland regions. The tufts of its pretty silky heads waving in the wind add beauty to the wildest districts. But lately bunches of its silvery threads were presented by troops of rosy Welsh children on the lookout for tourists amidst their own mountain passes. Various attempts have been made to utilize its silky down and to substitute it for cotton, but without success. The fibres are too rigid, and are shorter than those of cotton, and lack the knack of twisting properly which is the peculiarity of the real cotton plant, and in which it is unrivalled. In the districts where this cotton grass grows, however, it is collected by the poor inhabitants for stuffing pillows; but it absorbs moisture, and is not really good for this purpose Candle and lamp-wicks are made from it where it grows, but on the whole it cannot be considered a useful plant, and is only worth notice on account of its beautiful and graceful appearance which we all must admire.

BULRUSH.

SCIRPUS LACUSTRIS.

THIS handsome curious plant is often seen growing on the banks of our rivers and lakes. It belongs to the family *Cyperaceæ;* and is a representative of rushes of many and various kinds. It grows in clear stagnant water; but when its long stems are cut down, with its dark brown velvety spikes, they readily dry up and form beautiful objects of adornment for a long time. At this period, when it has become the fashion to cover our walls with china and other works of art, a number of these handsome spikes with their leaves attached are very effective around a high mantel-shelf or panel containing china; and it is a suitable addition to the large antique vases, with which our corridors and rooms are now adorned, to put bunches of these Bulrushes and other plants of the same order into each vase, as they require no care and no moisture. The reed-mace, *Typha Latifolia*, is sometimes called the Bulrush, but erroneously. The stems of this handsome plant are used for making the bottoms of chairs, mats, and other things of the sort. Coopers use them largely for placing between the staves of casks. Large quantities are brought from the marshy districts of Holland, where they grow, for this purpose, being first dried in the sun and tied up in bundles. The old name for the Bulrush was "bumbles." Gerarde, the old herbalist, tells us that "the tender leaves that be next the root make a convenient ointment against the biting of the spider called *Phalangium*."

The Bulrush recalls to our minds the extensive domestic use of rushes in ancient times, when even the process of weaving them into mats was unknown, and when the floors were daily strewed with fresh-gathered rushes; sometimes, be it said, without removing the accumulated litter of days from beneath, thereby outraging every law of health, then so little known or regarded. We can imagine, if the practice were cleanly and carefully carried out, it would not be unpleasant in the summer time. It still obtains, as we have said, on certain days in Norwich Cathedral, when rushes and the sweet-scented flag are strewn as of old; and we believe that until very lately the floors of some of the old colleges at Oxford were innocent of rugs or carpets, and knew no covering but the green and fragrant rush.

SWEET-FLAG—SWEET SEDGE.
ACORUS CALAMUS.

It is, perhaps, well to conclude our selection of Wild Flowers with one which is worth notice for qualities that do not directly address the eye. Beauty of form and colour are not alone the attractions of the vegetable kingdom, and, as with many other good things in life, we do not become aware of their excellence on a superficial acquaintance. The charming qualities of this our last specimen are undiscovered until we seek for them; not in fact until we have gathered it, and bruised it in our fingers. Then comes forth the pleasant fragrance which gives it its special character. It is a reed-like plant with a creeping horizontal stem. From this springs many deep green sword-shaped leaves about three feet long. In the midst of all is a leaf-like stem, from below the point of which comes a cylindrical, or rather a conical, spadix of greenish flowers, which are so densely packed together, that the stalk is quite hidden. It grows abundantly in the eastern counties of England, on the banks of rivers, and was used formerly for strewing the churches on festival days; the custom is, I believe, still preserved in the cathedral in Norwich on certain occasions. The very aromatic smell of this plant is singular amongst our native species. This property has, as might be expected, been made available in medicine. The roots have a strong aromatic smell and a warm pungent taste, consequently they have been prescribed in many ailments where slight stimulants seemed necessary. They constitute the *Calamus Aromaticus* of the shops.

Having now gone over the allotted collection of Wild Flowers, endeavouring to chronicle the chief attractions and virtues of each, I can but feel how little has been said when compared with all that remains unsaid, but felt. I have hesitated in making these little sketches many a time, because I had not the courage to pass by others rudely, whose claims to notice seemed as great as any I have chosen. The whole field of Nature lies before us; I can but hope that if there have been some interesting thoughts suggested by these our selected examples, they may but be inducements to still further study of the forms and functions of those beautiful creations on which so much of our welfare and happiness depends.

> "Blame me not, laborious band,
> For the idle flowers I brought;
> Every aster in my hand
> Comes back laden with a thought."—EMERSON.

INDEX.

	PLATE	FIG.	PAGE
Aconitum Napellus	ii	1	7
Acorus Calamus	xviii	4	149
Adonis autumnalis	i	4	4
Althæa officinalis	v	3	34
Anagallis arvensis	xiv	6	119
Anemone nemorosa	i	3	3
Anemone, Wood	i	3	3
Anthemis nobilis	x	4	85
Antirrhinum majus	xiii	5	110
Aquilegia vulgaris	i	6	6
Arrowhead, Common	xviii	2	143
Arum maculatum	xviii	3	144
Aster, Sea	x	2	83
Aster Tripolium	x	2	83
Atropa Belladonna	xiii	2	104
Bedstraw, Yellow	ix	4	76
Bee Orchis	xvi	3	130
Bellis perennis	x	5	79
Bindweed, Great	xii	1	96
Bindweed, Sea	xii	2	97
Bitter-sweet	xiii	3	107
Black Bryony	xv	5	126
Black Whortleberry	xi	1	88

INDEX.

	PLATE	FIG.	PAGE
Bladder-wort	xiv	1	115
Blood Geranium	v	4	38
Bryonia dioica	vii	5	59
Bryony, Black	xv	5	126
Bryony, Red or Wild	vii	5	59
Buckbean	xi	6	95
Bugloss, Viper's	xii	5	98
Bulrush	xviii	6	147
Burnet Rose, Common	vii	4	52
Butomus umbellatus	xviii	1	142
Buttercup	i	1	1
Callitriche verna	xv	3	132
Calluna vulgaris	xi	3	90
Caltha palustrus	ii	2	8
Campanula rotundifolia	x	6	86
Campion, Red	iv	4	30
Carnation	iv	3	29
Chamomile	x	4	85
Chicory	x	1	82
Chrysoplenium alternifolium	viii	2	63
Cichorium Intybus	x	1	82
Cinquefoil, Creeping	vii	2	54
Clematis Vitalba	i	2	2
Clove-pink	iv	3	29
Clover, Strawberry	vi	2	46
Codlins and Cream	vi	5	55
Colchicum autumnale	xvii	6	140
Columbine	i	6	6
Convolvulus sepium	xii	1	96
Convolvulus Soldanella	xii	2	97
Cotton Grass, Common	xviii	5	146
Cowslip	xiv	4	117
Crane's-bill, Red	v	4	38
Creeping Cinquefoil	vii	2	54
Creeping Loose-strife	xiv	5	119
Crithmum maritimum	viii	6	66
Crowfoot, Bulbous	i	1	1

INDEX.

	PLATE	FIG.	PAGE
Cuckoo-pint	xviii	3	144
Daffodil, or Daffy-down-dilly	xvi	6	134
Daisy	x	5	79
Deadly Nightshade	xiii	2	104
Dianthus Caryophyllus	iv	3	29
Dipsacus Fullonum	ix	6	77
Dog Rose, Common	vii	3	47
Draba verna	iii	2	18
Drosera rotundifolia	iv	1	26
Dwale	xiii	2	104
Dyer's Woad	iii	1	17
Early Orchis	xvi	1	128
Echium vulgare	xii	5	98
Elder	ix	2	73
Elecampane	x	3	84
Epilobium angustifolium	vi	5	55
Erica tetralix	xi	2	89
Eriophorum angustifolium	xviii	5	146
Eryngium maritimum	viii	5	64
Euphorbia Peplis	xv	2	122
Evening Primrose	vi	6	56
Flag, Sweet	xviii	4	149
Flag, Yellow or Water	xvi	5	132
Flax	iv	5	31
Flowering Rush	xviii	1	142
Fly Orchis	xvi	4	131
Forget-me-not	xii	6	99
Fritillaria Meleagris	xvii	5	138
Fritillary, Common	xvii	5	138
Fuller's Teasle	ix	6	77
Furze	vi	4	42
Galium Assarine	ix	5	67
Galium verum	ix	4	76
Gentian, Spring	xi	5	94
Gentiana verna	xi	5	94

INDEX.

	PLATE	FIG.	PAGE
Geranium, Blood	v	4	38
Geranium Robertianum	v	5	39
Geranium sanguineum	v	4	38
Germander Speedwell	xiii	4	108
Glaucium luteum	ii	5	15
Glaux maritima	xiv	2	116
Globe Flower	i	5	5
Golden Saxifrage	viii	2	63
Goose-Grass	ix	5	67
Gorse	vi	4	42
Grape Hyacinth	xvii	2	137
Grass of Parnassus	iv	2	37
Great Bindweed	xii	1	96
Great Mullein	xiii	6	111
Ground Ivy	xii	4	114
Harebell	x	6	86
Heart's Ease	iii	6	24
Heath	xi	2	89
Heather	xi	3	90
Helianthemum vulgare	iii	4	22
Henbane	xiii	1	102
Herb Robert	v	5	39
Hogsbean	xiii	1	102
Holly	xi	4	92
Holly, Sea	viii	5	64
Honeysuckle	ix	3	74
Horn Poppy, Yellow	ii	5	15
House Leek	vii	6	60
Hulm	vi	4	42
Hyacinth, Grape	xvii	2	137
Hyacinthus nonscriptus	xvii	1	136
Hyacinth, Wild	xvii	1	136
Hydrocotyle vulgaris	viii	4	64
Hyoscyamus niger	xiii	1	102
Hypericum calycinum	iv	6	35
Hypericum, Large-flowered	iv	6	35
Ilex Aquifolium	xi	4	92

INDEX.

	PLATE	FIG.	PAGE
Inula Helenium	x	3	84
Iris pseudacorus	xvi	5	132
Isatis tinctoria	iii	1	17
Ivy, Ground	xii	4	114
Lathyrus aphaca	vi	3	53
Lavatera arborea	v	1	32
Lavatera, Sea	v	1	32
Leek, House	vii	6	60
Lily, Snakeshead	xvii	5	138
Lily, Turk's-cap	xvii	4	139
Lily, White Water	ii	3	10
Lilium Martagon	xvii	4	139
Linum usitatissimum	iv	5	31
Lonicera Periclymenum	ix	3	74
Loose-strife, Creeping	xiv	5	119
Loose-strife, Purple	vii	1	58
Lords and Ladies	xviii	3	144
Lychnis Diurna	iv	4	30
Lysimachia Nummularia	xiv	5	119
Lythrum Salicaria	vii	1	58
Mallow, Marsh	v	3	34
Mallow, Musk	v	2	33
Mallow, Tree	v	1	32
Malva moschata	v	2	33
Man Orchis	xvi	2	129
Marsh Mallow	v	3	34
Marsh Marigold	ii	2	8
Marsh Pennywort	viii	4	64
Marsh Saxifrage	viii	1	61
Marsh Trefoil	xi	6	95
Meadow Saffron	xvii	6	140
Menyanthes trifoliata	xi	6	95
Military Orchis	xvi	2	129
Mistletoe	ix	1	69
Moneywort	xiv	5	119
Monkshood	ii	1	7
Mullein, Great	xiii	6	111

INDEX.

	PLATE	FIG.	PAGE
Muscari racemosum	xvii	2	137
Musk Mallow	v	2	33
Myosotis palustris	xii	6	99
Narcissus pseudonarcissus	xvi	6	134
Nasturtium officinale	iii	3	19
Nepeta glechoma	xii	4	114
Nettle, Common	xv	4	124
Nightshade, Deadly	xiii	2	104
Nightshade, Woody	xiii	3	107
Nuphar Lutea	ii	4	12
Nymphæa alba	ii	3	10
Œnothera biennis	vi	6	56
Old Man's Beard	i	2	2
Ononis spinosa	vi	1	45
Ophrys apifera	xvi	3	130
Ophrys muscifera	xvi	4	131
Orchis, Bee	xvi	3	130
Orchis, Early	xvi	1	128
Orchis, Fly	xvi	4	131
Orchis, Man or Military	xvi	2	129
Orchis mascula	xvi	1	128
Orchis militaris	xvi	2	129
Oxalis acetosella	v	6	41
Papaver Argemone	ii	6	13
Parnassia palustris	iv	2	37
Parnassus, Grass of	iv	2	37
Parsnip, Water	viii	3	62
Pea, Yellow	vi	3	53
Pennywort, Marsh	viii	4	64
Pheasant's Eye	i	4	4
Pimpernel	xiv	6	119
Plantago major	xv	1	120
Plantain	xv	1	120
Poor Man's weather-glass	xiv	6	119

INDEX.

	PLATE	FIG.	PAGE
Poppy, Prickly	ii	6	13
Poppy, Yellow Horn	ii	5	15
Potentilla reptans	vii	2	54
Prickly Poppy	ii	6	13
Primrose	xiv	3	116
Primrose, Evening	vi	6	56
Primula officinalis	xiv	4	117
Primula vulgaris	xiv	3	116
Purple Loose-strife	vii	1	58
Purple Spurge	xv	2	122
Ranunculus bulbosus	i	1	1
Red Bryony	vii	5	59
Red Campion	iv	4	30
Red Crane's-bill	v	4	38
Rest Harrow	vi	1	45
Robert, Herb	v	5	39
Rock Cist	iii	4	22
Rock Rose	iii	4	22
Rosa canina	vii	3	47
Rose, Common Burnet	vii	4	52
Rose, Common Dog	vii	3	47
Rosa spinosissima	vii	4	52
Rush, Flowering	xviii	1	142
Saffron, Meadow	xvii	6	140
Sagittaria sagittifolia	xviii	2	143
St. John's Wort	iv	6	35
Sambucus nigra	ix	2	73
Samphire	viii	6	66
Saxifraga Hirculus	viii	1	61
Saxifrage, Golden	viii	2	63
Saxifrage, Marsh	viii	1	61
Scilla verna	xvii	3	138
Scirpus lacustris	xviii	6	147
Scutellaria Galericulata	xii	3	113
Sea Aster	x	2	83
Sea Bindweed	xii	2	97

	PLATE	FIG.	PAGE
Sea Holly	viii	5	64
Sea Milkwort	xiv	2	116
Sempervivum Tectorum	vii	6	60
Sium angustifolium	viii	3	62
Skull-cap, Common	xii	3	113
Snakeshead Lily	xvii	5	138
Snapdragon	xiii	5	110
Solanum Dulcamara	xiii	3	107
Sorrel, Wood	v	6	41
Speedwell, Germander	xiii	4	108
Spring Gentian	xi	5	94
Spring Squill	xvii	3	138
Spurge, Purple	xv	2	122
Squill, Spring	xvii	3	138
Starwort, Water	xv	3	123
Stratiotes aloides	xv	6	127
Strawberry Clover	vi	2	46
Sundew	iv	1	26
Sweet Flag or Sweet Sedge	xviii	4	149
Tamus communis	xv	5	126
Teazle, Fuller's	ix	6	77
Traveller's Joy	i	2	2
Tree Mallow	v	1	32
Trifolium fragiferum	vi	2	46
Trollius Europæus	i	5	5
Turk's-cap Lily	xvii	4	139
Ulex Europæus	vi	4	42
Urtica dioica	xv	4	124
Utricularia vulgaris	xiv	1	115
Vaccinium Myrtillus	xi	1	88
Verbascum Thapsus	xiii	6	111
Veronica Chamædrys	xiii	4	108
Vetchling, Yellow	vi	3	53
Viola odorata	iii	5	22
Viola tricolor	iii	6	24
Violet, Sweet	iii	5	22

INDEX.

	PLATE	FIG.	PAGE
Viper's Bugloss	xii	5	98
Virgin's Bower	i	2	2
Viscum Album	ix	1	69
Water-cress	iii	3	19
Water Flag	xvi	5	132
Water Lily, White	ii	3	10
Water Lily, Yellow	ii	4	12
Water Parsnip	viii	3	62
Water Soldier	xv	6	127
Water Starwort	xv	3	123
Way-bread	xv	1	120
White Water Lily	ii	3	10
Whitlow Grass	iii	2	18
Whortleberry, Black	xi	1	88
Wild Bryony	vii	5	59
Wild Hyacinth	xvii	1	136
Willow Herb	vi	5	55
Wind Flower	i	3	3
Woad, Dyer's	iii	1	17
Wolf's-bane	ii	1	7
Wood Anemone	i	3	3
Woodbine	ix	3	74
Wood-sorrel	v	6	41
Woody Nightshade	xiii	3	107
Yellow Bedstraw	ix	4	76
Yellow Flag	xvi	5	132
Yellow Pea	vi	3	53
Yellow Vetchling	vi	3	53
Yellow Water Lily	ii	4	12

RICHARD CLAY & SONS, LIMITED, LONDON & BUNGAY.

29

www.ingramcontent.com/pod-product-compliance
Lightning Source LLC
Chambersburg PA
CBHW020830230426
43666CB00007B/1168